Using the Runes

A fascinating insight into this often-neglected but important area of the occult.

USING THE RUNES

by

D. Jason Cooper

THE AQUARIAN PRESS
Wellingborough, Northamptonshire

First published August 1987

British Library Cataloguing in Publication Data

Cooper, D. Jason
    Using the runes.
    1. Runes   2. Occult sciences
    I. Title
    133.3'34   BF1623.R89

    ISBN 0-85030-568-3

The Aquarian Press is part of the
Thorsons Publishing Group

Printed and bound in Great Britain

10 9 8 7 6 5 4 3 2 1

CONTENTS

Dedication:

To Nevill Drury and G. M. Glaskin,
Who brought Australian occult writing in from the cold

CHAPTER ONE

The Origin of the Runes

Our word 'rune' comes from a proto-Germanic root that meant, originally, 'to roar'. Over time it has evolved through the Old Norse run (secret writing), the Gothic runa (secret, whisper), Old English roun and rowan, and on into the modern English rune and the German runen. The core of meaning of all these words is 'whispered secret'.

In this book we will be looking at the runes as the magical alphabet used by the Germanic tribes of pre-Christian Europe for both magic and ordinary writing (e.g. in poems and legal documents). They are characterized by their angular shape, which distinguishes them from all other alphabets in the world, and have been seen in various forms of alphabet, each alphabet using different number of individual runes.

Mythically, the runes are associated with Odin (or Wotan or Wodan), the god of inspiration, battles, wisdom, and death. It is significant that Odin didn't invent the runes, but won them through a trial; he was hung for nine days and nights, wounded by a spear. The significance of this rite we will examine later.

The historical origin of the runes is, if anything, shrouded in even more mystery than their mythical origins. Attempts have been made by scholars to identify the runes from any one of a number of alphabets in use between the sixth century BC and the fifth century AD. In particular, the Greek and Latin alphabets in both their capital and cursive forms have been used as potential models for the runes.

One theory suggests that the runes were developed by the Goths from the Etruscan alphabet in about the first or second century BC. The Etruscans were a people who lived in the northern parts of the Italian peninsula, and at the time in question the Goths lived in adjacent

Germano-Austrian territories. In support of this theory, scholars have pointed to a number of inscriptions which were written in the Gothic language but in the Etruscan script.

A very different theory suggests that the runes evolved from the Hallristingnor carvings. These carvings appear to have been done in the later Stone Age or early Bronze Age and have been found in various parts of northern Italy, southern Germany, and Austria. Several of these carvings have the same shape as runes.

As should be becoming clear, scholars face certain insurmountable problems in trying to determine the origin of the runes. In particular, they face a lack of original or sample material. The earliest existing inscriptions are no older than about AD 400. And of the sources we do have, most are inscriptions and charms, of which only between 4,000 and 5,000 exist. In addition, there are only a handful of manuscripts written in the runes.

Even with this small sample there are other problems. Something over 2,500 of the inscriptions come from Sweden. The rest are from scattered places in Norway, Denmark, Britain, Iceland, the North Sea Islands, and down through France, Germany, Austria, and even the USSR. So there is little hope of gathering a substantial amount of material on the runes in any one area.

It's little wonder, then, that so much of modern scholarship is held together with the glue of speculation.

Nevertheless, there are some general outlines of runic history we *can* be certain of, and these by themselves make for fascinating considerations. For example, an earlier origin rather than later is suggested by the fact that the earliest inscriptions we have are written from right to left. It is only the oldest alphabets, such as the Hebrew, that are written in this direction. However, this could be pure imitation, rather than an indicator of true age.

Over time and in different places, several versions of the runic alphabet have emerged as letters were added and then dropped again. There are three major variants of the runes and a number of minor versions.

The oldest of the major forms of runic alphabets is the Common or Germanic futhark. Consisting of twenty-four letters, it derives the name 'futhark' from the fact that the first six letters are 'f', 'u', 'th', 'a', 'r', and 'k'—futhark. It was most commonly used in northern continental Europe between fifth and eighth centuries AD. Its letters were divided into three groups of eight, each group being called an *aettir* or family. Each aettir was attributed to a deity, Freyja, Heimdall, and Tiwaz (or Tyr). We'll be looking at this in more detail later on.

The second major variant of the runes is the Anglo-Saxon futhark. This was used in Britain between the fifth and twelfth centuries AD. Until about AD 900 it had twenty-eight letters, and after that it had thirty-three. The additional letters were needed to represent sounds that occurred in Old English but did not occur in the continental tongue. Two runes in modified form nearly made it into the English alphabet. However, the Norman influence cut short the careers of edh [ᛞ] and yogh [ᛉ]. The only other changes the Anglo-Saxon futhark made was to alter some of the names of the runes and to slightly alter their shapes.

The third and last major form of futhark is the Scandinavian or Norse. Used in Scandinavia and Iceland, it was most in use between the fifth and twelfth centuries AD and we have more examples of writing in this futhark than in any other.

Strangely enough, although Norse had even more sounds than Old English, this futhark has only sixteen runes. This is because each rune does double or triple duty. For example, one rune stood for both 'k' and 'g'. It worked in the same way that our 'c' can sound like an 's' or a 'k', only in this case both 's' and 'k' would have been dropped from the alphabet.

Any further futharks tend to be no more than cryptographic representations of one of the three variants. The tent runes, dotted runes, and twig runes are all examples of this.

The spread of these runes shows how very far the Germanic people travelled. The feat becomes even more remarkable when we consider that they were originally an Indo-Iranian people who had in turn migrated into India and Iran from some unknown region.

But such a wide spread perhaps should not surprise us. The Germanic tribes, from Iceland to Germany-Austria, were noted by friend and foe alike as individualists, travellers, explorers, and plunderers. They were a rough people often contemptuous of death. They consigned people who died of old age and disease (rather than in battle) to Niflheim and the fortress of Hel. They admired the man who faced death with a joke or defiance. The hardships of exploration or mass migration meant little to them. In groups they made their way over the majority of Europe and on to North America and left the records we now have.

This expanse of area helps explain the variations in the runes. After all, rather less stress and better communications saw splits in Christianity, first between Catholic and Orthodox, and then between Catholic and Protestant. But there is a better explanation of the changes than this.

It has been debated between scholars how deeply the use of the runes went. Some have held that their use was confined to inscriptions, charms and talismans, and only rarely in poems or legal documents. Others have argued that the runes were probably widely used in documents and similar writings. I agree with the latter suggestion. It would seem probable that any documents written in the runes would be written on bark or paper, and could easily be lost or destroyed, and that destruction would be probable. The Christian church was quite meticulous in destroying such things.

Moreover, if the runes were purely magical, there would be little need for variations in the basic futhark. The language in which magic is couched can easily be stylized so changes in the common tongue are not reflected in inscriptions. Moreover, in purely magical symbols there is a reluctance to make any alterations—note how long the zodiac symbols have remained unchanged. With more practical symbols, there is a higher chance of change.

When looking to see which of the three major variants is the original, this same evidence points to the Germanic futhark. It is unlikely that the Scandinavian futhark is the original, because letters have different sounds attached to them—like our 'c' or 's' and 'h' becoming 'sh'—tends to develop in the later part of the alphabet's history. The Saxon futhark is unlikely because so many of the runes are clearly derived from each other, just as our 'g' is derived from 'c' and 'j' is derived from 'i' and 'w' from 'u'. This, too, is a sign of an alphabet in its mature stages. Thus, the Germanic futhark would be indicated as the eldest.

In addition, the Germanic futhark is symbolically the richest. The division of the runes into aettirs allows more use of symbolism than in either of the other two futharks. This, too, supports the suggestion that this futhark was the central one.

In figure 1.1 we have each of the three major variants of the futharks. Other variants often depend on cryptography, and that of the Germanic futhark's three aettirs. Each rune is given a numerical value from what position it holds in its aettir, so that the first rune of the second aettir is 2/1, the fifth rune of the third aettir is 3/5, and so on. Then all you need is some method of putting the combinations of two numbers together. This is exactly what the twig, tent, and tree runes do. The code isn't hard to break, but it can be so easily disguised in everyday things like tapestries and embroidery that people are often slow to realize there's a coded message to break in the first place.

The use of these runes continued unabated until at least AD 1,000. During the 400 years up to then, the Christians were making converts in the pagan north. Much has been made of their sword and fire conversions, but there was more to the story than this. It was the upper classes who converted first, and their major motivations seem to have centred on the belief that Christianity offered a more secure map of what awaited them in the next world. The middle classes and lower classes were still almost entirely pagan in many areas.

The pagan gods were worshipped openly until the twelfth century and traces of runic use survived until the seventeenth century underground. It is even possible to suggest aspects of runic lore may have continued to the present day. It may be fashionable to down-play the continuity of underground thought, but it may be time for such concepts to be reappraised.

I am not suggesting that runic lore or the mythology was handed down in its entirety or even unchanged. I am suggesting that aspects of that lore may have continued to the present day intact. Note, for example, the sticks carved with runes which served as perpetual calendars. These were in used in both Norway (where they were called *primstaves*) and Denmark (where they were called *rimstocks*) as late as the nineteenth century.

But only aspects of runic lore survived. The binding force of organization and the continuity of initiation seem to have totally or almost totally deserted the cultus. There was no mass-organized underground keeping the pagan gods alive. There were simply people who kept the bits of runic lore or mythology they could make quick and practical use of, and a few who kept some part of the lore alive on a tenuous but rather better organized basis.

In this we should make note of the fact that there was a continued use of the runes throughout the Mediaeval Ages. Originally used openly, the Church declared their use a danger to the soul and forbade their use. But there appeared oddly-crossbeamed houses and house- and mason-marks which all showed runic shape to as late as the seventeenth century.

In southern Germany the Church also forbade the use of the name 'Woden's day' or *Wodenstag* (our Wednesday) and replaced it with *Mittwoch* or Midweek. These actions indicate a profound fear of a belief that should have been eliminated. It indicates the new beliefs were more a veneer than a reality. The royal houses may have converted easily, but the bulk of population was slower to do so.

Despite the powers of politics, inquisitions, and edicts, the runes had survived. What they couldn't survive was not an enemy, but a force that didn't even care if they existed. Like many methods of occult knowledge the runes required long study and only the most promising youths were chosen for the rigorous training their use requires. When the industrial revolution came, that time was no longer there; too many people, especially young people, were off to find their fortunes in the factories. The social structure that supported the trainees was collapsing rapidly.

In these conditions it is not surprising that the most easily grasped and immediately useful elements were the ones to survive. It should also follow that the customs and knowledge of the old ways were strongest where the disruption of the industrial revolution was least. When we do look, we see this is indeed the case; it was in the country areas, not the cities, that the old ways survived. Indeed, this is a general principle that applies all across Europe—Leyland did not find Tuscany witches in any large cities.

Moreover, as is the case so many times, it did not take long for people to seek what they had lost or thrown away. When the occult began to interest people again, many individuals and groups in Scandinavia, northern Europe, and Britain tried to revive runic and mythical lore. In some cases royal houses tried to mount the bandwagon, as Kaiser Wilhelm I and II did in Germany.

Most of the constructions of these occultists were highly fanciful, and the runes were often tied into any occult theory that was currently in vogue.

One interesting revival of the runes in the nineteenth century creates what might be called a fourth furthark. Like many of his contemporaries, Guido von List spent half his time with the occult and the other half with visionary politics. He had a system of eighteen runes which he declared to be the original system, all others being corruptions. His textual evidence was the mythic edda (poem) in which Odin is said to have won the runes. In that poem eighteen runes were mentioned.

The nineteenth century saw not only the peak of materialism in mid-century, but by the end of the century saw a revival of transcendental thought such as had not been seen since the days of the pagans. But many of the theories were untenable. Runes were tied to Atlantis, Antedeluvian worlds, the Bible or Jesus (who for some was a blond-haired, blue-eyed Aryan), and so on. It was a time when anthropology was a great rack to hang on any hat, and many occultists were quite willing to supply false evidence to support their theories.

Some of the work was silly, some of it was very good, and some of it, unfortunately, was tied to the *völkisch* movement.

The world *volk* translates literally as 'folk', but the words do not translate exactly. Where both words indicate an interest in traditional costumes, dances, music, stories, beliefs, and festivals, the German term carries a connotation of racism and elitism. The *völkisch* movement took root in Germany and the Austrian part of Austria-Hungary in the middle nineteenth century. It was mostly made up of men and a lesser number of women who rented private rooms in hotels, gave lectures on runes, Germanic culture, mythology, or pseudo-anthropology, had dinners and initiations, and then went home. Some went so far as to paint themselves blue, dress in animal skins and brandish swords in imitation of berserks. These manifestations of the *völkisch* movement were silly and no worse than similar beliefs of French, Italian, American, or Spanish greatness that existed at the same time.

But the *völkisch* movement contained some men of real ability and uncanny evil. They were not, as has been asserted, the raw material from which Hitler formed his movement, they were the men who created Hitler. Though a full exposition on this topic falls outside the scope of this volume, we will have to spend some time on it if only because Hitler has a known role in the runes and the occult, and we should set out exactly what this is. To do that we will have to explore the *Thule Gesellschaft*.

The Thule was founded in the nineteenth century but never amounted to much until Rudolf von Sebottendorff took control of it in 1917. Working with a war veteran, Walter Nauhaus, von Sebottendorff initiated thirty members in August 1917 and by November that year had 1,500 members. It was then he ordered his members to support, infiltrate, and/or bankroll almost any right-wing group that hated the Jews.

A few months after the programme of infiltration (which doubled as a covert membership drive), von Sebottendorff had different members create fronts. These various groups attracted members of various clubs which studied such topics as German heritage or occult anthropology. Likely prospects were then brought into the Germanenorden and, if they proved their worth there, were then initiated into the Thule group. The Thule group operated behind the Germanenorden in much the same way the R.R. et A.C. operated behind the Hermetic Order of the Golden Dawn.

Two of the front organizations are important. These are the 'Committee of Independent Workingmen' led by Anton Drexler and the 'Political Worker's Circle', led by Karl Harrer. These were merged to form the German Labour Party, known by its initials of DAP. It was this party that Hitler would join and turn into the NSDAP, the Nazi's.

Hitler's role in the growth of that party was far less than he maintained in *Mein Kampf*. And though every historian of note who has dealt with the period has conclusively refuted one significant aspect of Hitler's assertions or another, few have bothered to try to put together the real story. The myth of Hitler's constant speaking has been allowed to stand as the origin of his power. We have not yet fully grasped what was really happening in those early days in Munich.

Take, for example, the notion that Hitler had a talent for drawing together people whose talents complimented his own. Compare this to a list of some of the people who were in the DAP and in the Thule before Hitler was a member of either.

Ernst Rohm, leader of the Storm Troopers and essential to getting ex-servicemen to join the party; Heinrich Himmler, head of the SS and the *Deutsches Ahnernerbe*, the *de facto* Nazi occult bureau; Rudolf Hess, Deputy Führer until his still-unexplained flight to England in 1941; Alfred Rosenburg, Nazi apologist and idealogist; Richard Walter Darré, Hitler's Minister for Agriculture; Bernard Kohler, editor of the newspaper, the *Beobachter*, which supported, and was later bought by, the Nazi's; Bernhard Stemphle, a friar who helped ensure Hitler didn't have opposition from the Catholic Church in Bavaria as he had in Saxony; Friedrich Krohn, a man with a 2,500 book occult library, many of which books Hitler read, and possibly the man who really created the Nazi flag.

Two other men were especially important to Hitler's involvement with the DAP. Dietrich Eckart was a Thule and DAP member before Hitler. He had already stopped Rudolf Steiner's Anthroposophical Society from taking over the politics of Bavaria. He recognized the potential in Hitler and was Hitler's teacher in how to whip up a crowd's emotions by speeches and occult techniques. The other was Erich Ludendorff, Germany's *de facto* dictator in World War I. Ludendorff is not known to have been a member of the Thule, but he did attend meetings and his wife was a dues-paying member. It was Ludendorff who ordered Hitler's captain (Hitler was still in the army in 1919) to allow Hitler to join the DAP, get it organized, and expand it. Towards this, Hitler was provided with twenty gold marks per month and kept his salary for some months after he officially resigned from the army in order to join the new party.

Thus Hitler became a politican whose power was backed by a knowledge of the occult that exceeded any other politician's of the day except, perhaps, FDR.

Hitler saw potential support in the *völkisch* movement, and did not hesitate to use occult symbols and power to his ends. In this he used mainly the swastika and the double 's' rune for the SS. He led a movement which had an evangelical interest in the runes and the mythology in which they had existed. But it was a perverse interest which gloried in the blood of an heroic age but ignored the honour and personal sacrifice that had gone with it. Indeed, some would suggest that by turning the swastika around so that it travelled against the sun rather than with it, the Nazi's tapped occult forces that sealed their doom.

But because of Hitler, interest in the runes was laid aside for several decades. It was only in the seventies that they began to emerge again, and now have a significant number of students throughout the occult. Their strength lies in the fact that they are a practical magic, where 'a gift demands a gift' is a truism that always applies. They are a magic that allows no-one too much, and one should always keep in mind the philosophy of the runes when using them.

The Philosophy of the Runes

The notable thing about the runes is that they have such an ecological viewpoint. In this they differ sharply from the Kabbalah or the Judeo-Christian traditions of magic and ally much more closely with the Zoroastrian and Mithraic traditions and world views. Indeed, the runes are symbols of nature and natural forces. As in the Zoroastrian religion the concepts of the 'holy' and the 'bountiful' have not become wholly separated.

In runic philosophy there is no division between the natural order of things and the deity/ies which spawned it. And this feeling has much to do with the interest in the runes now entrenching itself in occult thought. The other-worldliness of the other main schools of Eastern and Western magic no longer wholly serve human feelings if, in fact, they ever did wholly serve those feelings.

The runes were a magic used largely by peasants, and peasants are too concerned with this world to spend too much time on any other. Their magic must provide something in hand, and any declaration that magic used to self-advantage must necessarily be evil will be dismissed. Equally, peasants understand there is no free lunch. The extra field cultivated meant a proportionate increase in work. The extra money you got for yourself by magic came with responsibilities to the community. And so on. A gift demanded a gift, and it was better not to pledge than to pledge overmuch.

Thus the scope of runic magic was circumscribed. It is little wonder, then, that we have no tales of runic mages using their powers to gain political position. What inscriptions we have are mainly aimed at some practical effect; they defend against enemies, they provide a better attack on enemies, they improve fertility and health, they protect the burial ground from invaders, they keep away demons, and so on.

This reflected the picture of the individual in Germanic mythology. Human beings were valued allies of the gods against the frost giants and stone giants. But they were neither the centre of the universe (as they were in Christianity) nor the measure of all things (as in modern materialism). Also, unlike Greek mythology, people did not become gods, as did Glaucon or Herakles. The human role was a fixed one, and it was only by performing that allotted role that human beings become perfected.

Moreover, Germanic mythology was based on concepts of purification and balance. Only by pure action and pure intent could a human being properly accede to the destiny given to them by the Norns. In a world where stark anonimity and bureaucracy threaten to swallow us, it is not surprising that the runes should make an appearance again. They were created in similar conditions of precarious existence of the individual and the community.

For just as the wandering tribes were threatened with destruction, so is the human 'tribe' seen to be threatened today. The runes offer the sort of comfort needed when facing an enemy who seems invincible.

In a time between the Ages of Pisces and Aquarius, we have turned to a more ancient magic than Christianity and its ilk. We have turned to questions of balance and purity in action, life, and motive. And for this, we have turned to the runes.

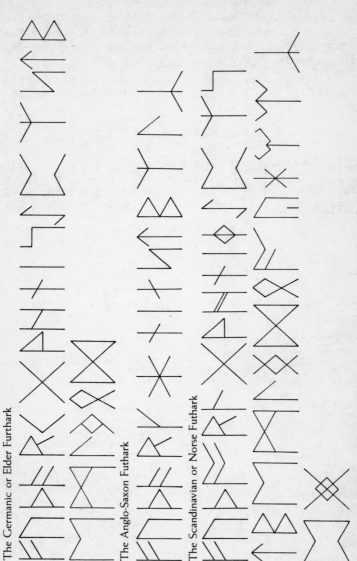

The Germanic or Elder Furthark

The Anglo-Saxon Futhark

The Scandinavian or Norse Futhark

Figure 1.1: The Three Major Futharks.

- Main area of use of the Scandinavian futhark

- Main area of use of the Germanic futhark

- Main area of use of the Anglo-Saxon futhark

○ - Byzantium: the Empire retained Vikings in the Emperor's personal bodyguard. Their height became proverbial. It was said they were all 'ten feet tall', and this expression was later used to identify great men.

↓ - arrows: Show direction of further exploration but not permanent settlement. Greenland is the most famous of these, and might constitute a permanent settlement had the lives of the settlers not been so miserable and their numbers so few. Germanic travellers also travelled along the Volga and the Black Sea. Indeed, Russia is named after the Germanic people, the Rus. Invading Germanic tribesmen further sacked and conquered areas of France, Spain, Northern Italy, and even Libya. These conquests, though, had little to do with the development of the runes or Germanic paganism.

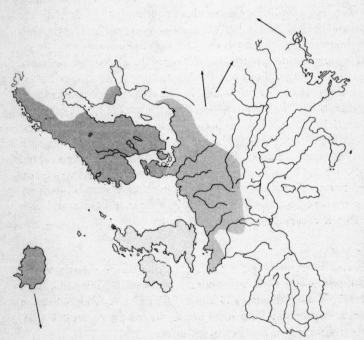

Figure 1.2: Distribution of Rune Use.

CHAPTER TWO

Myth and the Cult of Odin

When dealing with the mythology and cult activities of the pagans we have many of the same problems we have when studying the history of the runes, themselves. In many ways the problems are worse. We have only a small part of the whole body of myths. Many important images appear only once, and many deities are still almost wholly unknown. For example, we know almost nothing of Ull or Ullr, the archer and ski-god. Not only is the mythos incomplete, it is late, with most manuscripts dated about AD 1,000. However, by cross-referencing traditions, myths, and the runes themselves we can piece the picture together, however slowly.

It is now certain that the traditions recorded by Snorri Sturluson and others was a consistent tradition that covered the area of northern Europe, Britain, the North Sea Islands, Scandinavia, and Iceland. The tradition lasted from at least the Bronze Age to between the twelfth and seventeenth centuries AD. That is, the symbols we find carved in rock are the same that appear in the myths and they are clearly joined by unbroken tradition. With that in mind, we can begin to say with some confidence what happened in the Germanic cultus and what the esoteric meaning of their myths really was.

Odin

Odin was the central, but not the only, god of the runes. He was worshipped over a wide area under a plethora of names including Wodenaz, Wotan, Voden, or Odinn or Odhinn, and Woden. Even in Christian times many local royal houses traced their ancestry back to this god in one or another of his guises.

Tacitus, the Roman writer of the first century AD, described Odin as the Mercury of the Germanic tribes, and this description has been accepted ever since. It is based on the role of Odin as the psychopompous, or guide of the dead, which the two gods shared. This attribution was widely accepted, and when the Germanic tribes imitated the Roman calendar, Odin was assigned to the day of the week the Romans had assigned to Mercury. But any close examination of Odin shows this attribution to be incorrect. Odin, remember, was the god of battles and Mercury had no connection with war at all.

Odin is a god whose edges have been blurred by the history of the man and the cult, but we can still distinguish three layers to his image. There is the warrior-king who led his people on the wandering, found a permanent home for them, established laws, and was deified after his death. There is the shaman and cult creator who became the god of the dead and wisdom, and this figure is the one who ties with Mercurial attributes. Then there is the Allfather Odin, the god of hosts and warriors who would one day fall on the battlefields of ragnarok. In this last guise we have what seems to be the latest Odin, the one most remembered, but the one who was fast being replaced in the close of the pagan era.

The warrior-king was a chieftain of a wandering tribe who led his people through Europe and eventually settled in northern Europe or Scandinavia (Denmark or southern Sweden being the best guesses). There he founded a kingdom and promulgated laws for his now settled people. For a time his autocracy led to his overthrow by a Dane named Oller, but the myth of the overthrow and regaining of the throne is one of many myths alluded to but not preserved.

Like many of the lawgivers of his time, Odin was deified after his death. It is possible his personal attributes were merged with a previously existing local deity named *Od*. There is in fact a god of the same name mentioned as being the husband of Freyja, but who was said to have abandoned her and never takes part in the myths we still have. If there was a merging of man and deity, it is likely to have been aided by Odin's own shamanistic cult, which would have been one of the pillars to his rule—and could have been the origin of the myth of desertion and why Frigg (Odin's wife) shares a number of attributes with Freyja (Od's wife).

The image of Odin as a wandering shaman is a striking one, and one that can still be frightening. He was a tall, thin man with grey hair that fell in a wild tangle to his shoulders. He wore a cloak and a broad-rimmed hat that he pulled down low to hide the fact that he was missing one eye. The eye left intact was a piercing blue. He was accompanied by two familiars, a raven and a wolf. He was described as carrying either a spear or a blackthorn staff. In this image Odin is god of the dead and wisdom. Like many shamans, his functions include summoning the dead and interpreting their wishes.

The third layer of Odin, Allfather, shows how successful his original cult had become. The image of Allfather Odin fought Christianity for longer than many scholars would care to admit. But the role of Allfather was a conquest of the position of chief of the gods previously held by Tiwaz, Tiw, or Tyr.

Tyr is now remembered simply as a god of war, but the earliest version of his name, Tiwaz, is derived from an Indo-Iranian root which means, variously, *day* or *shining sky* or even *father sky*. The same root word entered Greek first as *Zayus* and later as *Zeus*. In Latin it became *Deus Pitar* or *Iuppiter*, our *Jupiter*. All Odin did was take over some of the characteristics of the earlier chief deity and push his rival into the background.

In this guise Odin and his two brothers, Vili and Ve, created the universe we live in. Odin in fact was the ninth creature created in the nine worlds of the universe. Nine is the most recurring number in Germanic mythology.

Like his shaman counterpart, Allfather has one eye, but his weapon is now *Gungnir*, a fabled spear made of beaten gold which never misses its mark, and with which he stirs up trouble and war among men. More, he is an all-seeing god, for from his chair *Valaskjalf* he sees everything and anything in creation. He also has two ravens, *Huginn* (thought) and *Muninn* (memory) who fly out over the world each day and then return to Odin and whisper in his ears what they've seen and heard.

This Odin is not a wanderer, but has a hall called *Valhalla*, the hall of the slain. Half the warriors who fall in battle are taken by the *Valkyries* to this hall. Every day there is battle in preparation for ragnarok. The slain are raised again in time for the feasting that occurs each night. This will continue until ragnarok itself comes to destroy the gods.

Like his shaman counterpart, Allfather is a sombre figure who seems little interested in the company of others—indeed, what company he prefers seems to be disreputable. But Allfather's grimness is a foreboding of doom, of the day when he would be fated to be devoured whole by Fenris the wolf. To forestall that day, he sought wisdom at any price. For example, he became one-eyed by giving up one eye to gain a draught of mead that made anyone who drank it a poet, and he shared this gift with men.

These are the images of Odin, and it must be said they do not always sit well with each other. A wanderer does not sit well with a god who enjoys stirring trouble among men with his spear, *Gungnir*. A being who preceded the universe does not sit well with one who is so much at its mercy.

As we have seen, these differences arise from layers of traditions, one added on top of the other. I suggest the core of these images was the physical man who lived any time between the sixth century BC and the fifth century AD (the times when the runes were thought to have arisen) and probably about the turn of the millenia. During his lifetime he led his people west and north, possibly from Asia if long parts of the trek were by rivers or sea, and settled his people as described. During his lifetime, possibly during an exile while Oller sat on the throne, he codified magical seals in use and probably added new ones, and created the first set of runes. This version may well have had eighteen characters; if so it is now lost to us, but its uses no doubt paralleled the Germanic futhark.

It is probable that during his time in exile he became the wanderer. The image of the psychopompous, shaman, and wanderer entered the popular imagination. With a shamanistic cult to back him, he regained the throne. After his death he was deified.

The cult was successful enough for the image of Odin to become chief of the gods by about AD 300 at the latest, replacing Tiwaz. Tiwaz, in turn, became simply a god of war, shorn of his duties as god of cosmic and personal justice. Many of the myths that had been ascribed to Tiwaz were now applied to Odin. For example, the myth of losing an eye for wisdom seems to have originally belonged to Tiwaz, with the Moon being the eye. It was bound with the phases of the moon.

But by 700 to 1,000 in this era, the cult of Odin was in decline. It had been, or soon would be, replaced by the cult of Thor, and in Sweden the cult of Thor was already being replaced by the cult of Freyer. The struggle with Thor's cult can be seen in the *Lay of Harbard* and the *Lokasenna*. In the former, Odin taunts a Thor who does not recognize him, and the two prove to have almost nothing in common and in fact have some areas of severe opposition. In the *Lokasenna*, Loki taunts each of the gods with their failings. Since the poem was late, some thought it a Christian fabrication, but there is a better interpretation to the poem. It seems that Thor, the only god Loki can't drag down to his level, is being extolled. His answer is the answer to the hard debates that the Christian missionaries were winning, particularly on the fate after death; 'Shut your mouth or I'll smash your head!'

But paganism eventually went into eclipse. Christianity dominated and the cult of Odin, like the cults of the other gods, went into hiding. Odin survives now only in the tradition of the leader of the wild hunt of Anglo-Saxon folklore.

In magical use, Odin is a multifaceted god. The clean lines of division applied to Greek and Egyptian gods have no place among the Germanic gods. Odin is more than Mercury, and less. He is not a god of healing, but he is the day-sky. Odin is a god of wisdom and he can be invoked for learning and understanding, anything to do with the dead, and to gain victory. He is the god of inspiration and poetry. He is a warrior, and represents leadership and authority. In this he is like Jupiter, but unlike Jupiter and unlike Tiwaz, Odin is not a god of justice. Finally, Odin is the god of the runes, and can be invoked for any aspect of dealing with them, as when divining.

But to fully understand both Odin and the use of the runes, we will have to examine Odin's cult.

The Cult of Odin

We know rather little about the religious and cultic activities of the Germanic pagans. We often depend on uncoordinated reports from a number of people with knowledge of similar societies who had rites that paralleled those of the Germanic peoples and from them we must extrapolate. Since Odin's cult is based on shamanism, we are fortunate, because shamanism is so widespread as to almost be a human universal. In addition, we do have knowledge of some of Odin's followers from external sources. So we are better placed to know this cult than, say, the cult of Balder, which we do not know for certain even existed.

A person learning to be a shaman would begin their training by following his or her teacher into the wilds to live off the land for a while. This would mean learning to survive by finding edible plants and being able to track and snare prey. They would have to learn to be able to tell the coming weather from such signals as the song of birds and the croak of frogs.

The teacher was normally a relative such as the parent of the same sex or a maternal uncle. In the myth of the creation of the world, Odin's mother is mentioned, and in another he mentions the woman's brother as the one who taught him. So we do have in the myths some elements of Odin's own training.

During the student's time in the wilds, he or she would be given exercises to do. Some of these would be in the form of tests, others were more like the formal exercises familiar in other schools of occultism. For example, the student would learn to put himself in ever deeper trances by rhythmic breathing, ecstatic dance, chants, and drugs. They would have to learn the magical formulas of words and, as part of that, how to write poetry in certain meters and scans that were thought to have magical power.

The student would also have to learn how to prepare his or her own tools. That would mean finding and preparing magical plants like the mandrake and the magic mushroom, learning how to dry animal entrails, carving magic wands, and so on. These various devices were used to make totemistic images, drugs and medicines, and so on.

But a major part of shamanistic learning would be meeting the magical forces of the world. It should be remembered that for shamanism throughout the world, nature is magical in the same way that a physicist sees it as formulas. Thus the student would have to converse with those forces in order to learn how to control them. This would mean meeting the force of wolves by talking to a wolf, to talk to the power of stones by speaking to a single stone, to talk to the winds in order to know their spirit, and so on.

Eventually one or more of these forces would become the guide of the student. These spirits would in many ways take over from the human teacher, teaching the shaman-to-be things his or her teacher might never have known. The shaman would never lose the guide for as long as the shaman lived. Odin, it would seem, chose or was chosen by the raven and wolf. Since the north wind was 'Od', it may be that 'Odin' is a magical name, not his true name at all, and it was probably with the deity of that wind that the man was fused in order to become a god.

All the studies of the shaman-to-be led to an ultimate test bound in the concept of death and rebirth. The word shaman itself derives ultimately from the Sanskrit word, *šrama*, which means 'religious experience'. The core of all shamanism is that experience, in which the initiate is put through physical trials such as being suspended from beams by leather thongs or hooks or is buried alive. He or she would have gone through preparation for this by ritual dance, fasting, chanting, and drugs. On the edge of death, he or she would look into a gap or chasm between this world and the world of the dead. Often this experience was accompanied by out-of-body experiences, and these were often in the form of one of the shaman's familiars.

Not all members of Odin's cults were fully-fledged shamans, however. Quite a few had only partial training. These were the berserks and the ennobled followers. The shamans sustained the cult, the berserks defended it, and the nobles funded it. And each had a distinct role to play when the cult was founded. Remember that at this time the tribes were in chaos and a single chieftain who knew how to take risks and succeed could reverse the fortunes of his entire tribe.

The shamans were those who were taught by Odin or his students.

The knowledge was passed down, and the shamans could offer eternal life to any who died in battle in service of Odin. In the early cult this seems to have been simply purification, a protection against the dragon that lived beneath the earth. In later times this after-life was formalized into the one at Valhalla.

Where previous gods, particularly the Vanir or fertility gods, buried their dead, the cult of Odin practised cremation. This in turn meant building a bier on which various protective and salutory runes could be carved. This explains why the inscriptions we have do not guide the dead. Any such inscriptions would have already been burned to protect the double, or soul, from the dragon *Nidhogg*.

Defending the faith were the berserks, fanatic warriors who shunned armour in preference to cloaks or animal skins. Indeed, they often fought naked except for a belt of hide. The name 'berserk' simply means 'bear shirt'. A few soldiers oblivious to personal wounds or coming death were essential when hosts were often outnumbered, and the berserks proved vital to the defence and spread of the cult. The berserks sustained the tribes in the difficult days of the wandering.

Berserks lived separate from others. They were normally bachelors who lived together in a barracks or commune and held all their property in common. When alone, they lived off the 'hospitality' of the people they imposed themselves upon.

But though vital to the community, the berserks were not fully trained. They could tattoo the runes on their skin or place them on their weapons, but they didn't know the full control of a shaman. Thus ex-berserks were often found to suffer from uncontrollable fits of rage that could cause death to people around them, even their families. Alcoholism seems to have been endemic, and a number of proverbs warned against the dangers of drunkenness, loose tongues, and boasting. But few berserks lasted into old age. When they grew older, they normally died on the battlefield.

The Mythology of the Runes

The shamanistic world view is consistent throughout the world. Moreover, it is as internally consistent as the major religions of the world. Shamanism, for example, has a central image of a world tree or pillar. In the Germanic mythology this role is taken by *Yggdrasil*, the world ash which spread its branches over all the nine worlds of creation. It sustained the life of the universe and would preside over the next universe when ours had died.

Odin gained his powers of the runes by hanging from Yggdrasil. This was his shamanistic initiation, and it is quite significant that myth has shifted the event from an ordinary tree to the world tree. Occulticly, the death can be paralleled to the myths of Jesus, Attis, and Dionysus, among others. One of the eddas gives the event as follows.

I hung from a windswept tree,
hung there for nine days and nights,
I was gashed, pierced with a spear,
I was an offering made to Odin.
Offered, myself to myself,
On that tree which no man knows,
Or where its roots still run.

No-one gave me bread,
No-one gave me drink from a horn,
I peered down into the worlds,
Down into the depths I peered and
Snatched up the runes.
Screaming, I took them.
Then I fell back.

Then I began to thrive,
Then my wisdom grew as
I prospered and was fruitful.
One word led to another,
One word led me to many words,
and one deed gained me many deeds.

Similar forms of initiation can be found all over the world, but in all other cases the sacrifice is to a god. Never before was the sacrifice to oneself (except Jesus Christ, which was the sacrifice of one part of a triple god to another). In terms of occult process, then, it seems clear Odin's intent was to become a god. In this it is also clear that the sacrifice resulted in the discovery, not the invention of the runes.

With what we know of Odin, and recalling the layers of development, we can suggest that the man was a shaman of the cult of Tiwaz. When he gained knowledge of the runes he tied all the disparate elements of instruction to those runes. This is why they have such an emphasis on natural powers. The runes in fact were a combination of various elements of that teaching. They included symbols long-used by the tribes which can still be seen today in the Hallristingnor carvings. Added to these were some letters from the Greek, Roman, and Etruscan alphabets. At points phonetic values were assigned purely because of similarity of shape. From this Odin was able to codify the shamanistic instruction as never before and found his cult.

What distinguished the cult from others was the use of the runes, the promise of protection from the dragon Nidhogg, and the cremation of the dead. The rest of the cult developed in ways we've already seen. But much of the mythology was kept, and the structure of that myth was carefully maintained.

The Germanic people were Aryans who had come from India and Iran. They kept some of the myths they'd known before the travellings. In particular, they preserved aspects of that stratum of Indo-Iranian thought seen in the Rg. Veda and the Zoroastrian Gathas. For example, in Germanic mythology the doom of the gods would come after three winters which had no intervening summer. The world would then be swept by the fires of *Muspell*. In Zoroastrian mythology the final battle between good and evil will take place after three years of winter with no intervening summer. When good has triumphed, all human beings past and present will pass through a river of molten metal which will purify or destroy all those people who are evil.

Again, in both Zoroastrian and Germanic thought the beginning of time sees two necessarily antagonistic forces which, by their contention, bring the universe we know into being. In both cases a sacred cow is intimately involved in this creation. In both cases the death of a giant who is hermaphroditic is involved. And in both cases the forces that gave rise to the universe will contend until the final days, and all small battles are a dress rehearsal for that final battle. In the mean time, the evil or chaotic forces are contained or imprisoned underground.

Not only the structure, but a large number of minor points also agree. For example, in Germanic mythology, Loki is said to come to the battle of ragnarok in a ship made from the nails of dead men. In Zoroastrianism the nails of the dead must be blessed lest they become useful to evil forces.

From this I began to re-examine the myths of the Germanic tribes as they'd come down to us. It would seem that those we now have are a late corruption of the originals. It would seem that originally ragnarok was a purification, after which the world was restored to its pristine state. Only later did it become a destruction of all the gods but a few. Indeed, some of the earlier concept is revealed by the fact that some of the gods' playing pieces were found in the grass by the sons of the gods after ragnarok; it is not a new world but the old one restored.

Individual myths then began to reveal the original, esoteric purpose in ritual or eschatological argument. From that I could then turn to the runes and examine their esoteric meaning in the light of this new information.

As has been mentioned, the runes were the central new technique of the cult of Odin. They were a codification of many of the techniques that had existed before, but gave them new direction. This means that the runes embody much of the original purpose of paganism, drawing out many distinctions that have been blunted in paganism's later days.

When this was done, the runes became easier to understand. Instead of a collection of symbols, they became a description of a type of magical process. For example, where the Hebrew alphabet is a series of symbols or sublimated pictures, the runes are a series of descriptions of forces and their propagation. They are a unique description of the magical world around us, and one that should be understood better.

In this work, we will be using an understanding of what the creation and ragnarok myths may have actually been to the early pagans.

Combined, it forms a two-part or two-act play in which Tiwaz and his two brothers join to create the universe out of the body of the hermaphroditic giant, Ymir. The world is set in its pristine state, but comes to decay.

Ragnarok then shows the redemption of that world. The fires of Muspell will purify it just as Zoroastrians consider fire to be the purifying element. What it will purify the world of is death and decay, just as molten metal will purify the world in Zoroastrian mythology. During ragnarok, Tiwaz was swallowed whole by the wolf Fenrir. But Vidar, his son, puts one foot on the lower jaw of the wolf and, with his hand forces the jaws of the wolf open, killing the animal and freeing his father. In the myth we have, Vidar breaks the wolf's jaws to revenge Odin, but nothing more is made of this unusual method of fighting.

Tiwaz, restored, then leads the world to redemption. More, that same battle sees Loki and Heimdall, who even in late versions of the myth are called 'those ancient enemies' have their final battle. The roles of both these gods have puzzled mythographers for many years. It would seem that their roles are of the eroding sea (Loki) and the shore (Heimdall). In the restored world, the shifting shorelines will no longer exist, just as Zoroastrianism similary suggests a restored world without some of the dangers and inconveniences we have known to date.

It is not possible to give a full description of the myths, but it is hoped the reader will take some time to examine these myths so that the use of the runes will be put in a proper context, as a unifying bond to a whole set of beliefs as worthy of our attention and respect as any other path of occultism.

And it is to the runes themsleves that we turn next.

CHAPTER THREE

The Esoteric Meaning of the Runes

As has been mentioned there are three main forms of futhark. In this book we'll be using the Germanic futhark of twenty-four letters and three aettirs. For each rune we will now examine its esoteric meaning. Each description is prefaced with details of that rune's major correspondences. Before going on to divination and magic you should be fully conversant with the contents of this chapter.

The Runes

Name: Feoh   *Number*: 1
Sound: F   *Colour*: Brown
Origin: Hallristingnor carving shaped—

Feoh refers to cattle as a domesticated beast, and hence to property, money, and creative value. This is one of the runes of the 'good things' of life. It should be remembered that cattle were essential to ancient societies, and they often had central roles to play in religions of the times. Indeed, cattle were often slaughtered during the feasts that generally accompanied religious holidays.

For example, in Zoroastrianism one of the holy books is devoted to a dialogue between the soul of domesticated cattle (a group soul, if you will) and Ahura Mazda, the deity of light. In this the soul asks where it shall find the 'good shepherd', the one who will treat the cattle well. Even today, Zoroastrians ritually slaughter cattle by holding them steady so incantations can be said and a log suspended from chains can be drawn back to then thump into the animal's head. This stuns the beast and drives any demons out of it. Similar methods were used by the Germanic pagans. Indeed, the rune is a pictograph from the top of a yoke through which the animal's horns are protruding.

This act of sacrifice was part of the pagan concept of responsibility. Those with wealth were those who provided more at the times of the feasts. This was not confiscation but the earning of a social and religious merit. Moreover, it ensured that even the poor were able to feed themselves on these days.

Thus the rune represents wealth and plenty, but also the distribution of the plenty. It is a sign of hope for all those in the society, but carries some measure of responsibility for those at its top.

Name:	Ur	*Number*: 2
Sound	U	*Colour*: Green
Origin:	Hallristingnor carving shaped—	

Where feoh was the symbol of domesticated cattle, this is the symbol of wild oxen. It recalls the primaeval cow of the Germanic myths, *Adumla*. In the beginning of all things the worlds of ice and fire contended. When they met a temperate zone was created, and in this there grew a brine. Adumla licked the brine and thus freed Odin's grandfather from it. The cow then nursed the father of the gods. This part of the myth recalls Zoroastrianism's group soul of the cattle, but it is much closer to the central myth of Mithrasism.

Mithras was the god of light who by killing the sacred cow let time and the universe begin. It was from the cow's blood, bones, and skin that various essential elements of civilization were gained, such as metal, grains, and so on. Mithras was himself a god not only of the Zoroastrians, but the Hindus (though he is called 'Mitra' or 'Mithra' in these cases).

In keeping with these various images, ur represents the wild and untamed side of the nature of cattle. It is the primal energies of creativity and fertility. But there is an element of danger involved with this rune. In this context it is important to remember that cattle were originally wild creatures. The rune itself shows the horns of a bull readying to charge.

It was possible to find wild cattle. Their capture was dangerous, but success could lead to a sudden addition to wealth. This could be through immediate slaughter or through breeding the animal with domesticated stocks and improving the blood stock.

This rune indicates great potential or power, but also danger from letting forces get out of control. For example, Mithras was admired not only for killing the bull but his heroic action of subduing it. In this it is worth noting that Mithras has often been compared with the pagan deity, Balder.

Name: Thorn   *Number*: 3
Sound: Th   *Colour*: White
Origin: Hallristingnor carving shaped— ↑

Thorn is the symbol of the ice demon that lived in the remotest parts of the forest and which fed on human flesh. Again, there are parallels with other cultures. Certain North American Indians feared the Wendigo, a very similar beast. Zoroastrianism, too, had a number of demons including ice demons.

In the context of Germanic paganism, this rune refers to the frost giants who always threatened the gods, as well as the ice demons, themselves. It should be remembered that in the pagan north population was often scarce, and people could go many days without meeting another human being. Fear of being frozen to death or being torn apart was a very real and immediate fear. It thus became a vital task of the shamans to understand the magical forces behind that fear, to understand the astral entities that could feed off and intensify it. It was this study that led to their understanding of these ice demons, an understanding that seems to have been far more acute to them than for other traditions.

This is a rune of attack and test. It can be used to attack an enemy and drive them insane. It can be used to test someone (including yourself) to see if they can overcome the fears they have. The form of this fear does not have to be the cold itself, or even be through the agency of those particular demons. It can be any aspect of physical danger or internal fears. For example, it is a rune that can be used to promote accidents or to make someone careless at exactly the wrong moment. It can also be used to see if one has the right to use the runes.

Name: Os   *Number:* 4
Sound: A to O   *Colour:* Purple
Origin: Hallristingnor rune shaped— ⇑

The word 'os' simply means 'god' or 'deity', and derives from the Indo-Iranian root, 'dayus'. This rune can refer to any deity, but normally applies specifically to Odin as the chief god of the runes.

Magically, the rune refers to divine power and the invocation of that power. This power is essentially neutral, but is generally held to be beneficent to human beings. This is a rune of luck and of the religious impulse in human beings. It is a pictograph of a pine tree, which is a symbol of immortality and divine beneficence. Part of this symbolism comes from the fact that pine trees are so obviously both male and female, but the herbal medicines gained from the tree may have helped with the symbolism as well.

This rune can be used as a general invocation of the beneficent powers of the universe, just as the rune thorn can be used to raise the chaotic elements. This rune is thus a useful rune of defence against obsession and accident. It can in fact be taken as a stylized picture of Odin standing with his cloak billowing in the wind, and this image does well to show the powers of this rune. Odin was a representation of supernatural powers which often appeared on the earth, and this is his rune. It is divine power invoked by or in human beings.

In this latter role, the rune is useful for creative work. It can be used to stimulate inspiration for such things as poetry, divination, speaking, and so on. In this way it can be an adjunct in works relating to social affairs, seduction, and other things which need quick work.

Name: Rad   *Number:* 4
Sound: R   *Colour:* Black
Origin: The Roman letter R

This rune is a symbol of a journey on horseback, which in turn is a poetic image for a ride into the underworld. It is a universal technique of shamans entering the world of the dead to be riding an animal. They never go there alone. Thus, Freyja rode a bird and Odin rode the eight-legged horse, *Sleipnir*. Sleipnir has been used as a symbol of four men carrying a coffin, but we do have cases of other eight-legged animals serving as familiars. For example, a cow born with residual front and back legs was to be the familiar of a shamanka until her husband unwittingly amputated the appendages.

Death is one of the essential features of a culture. The belief in an after-life, reincarnation, the burning or burial of the dead, and so on. Much of the doctrine relating to death is based on handling what the occultists call the etheric body and the shamans called the double. This is a non-material body which has an appearance similar to the physical body. Thus, Mithrasism is reincarnational but with some elements of single-life. Zoroastrianism is single-life but with some elements of reincarnation. Germanic mythology, however, was mainly single-life with reincarnation only just entering into the scheme of things in the late pagan period.

Lack of reincarnation seems to give rise to thoughts of the double more than reincarnation does. There is no obvious place for the soul to go and be neutralized. So where the cults of the Vanir buried their dead, the cult of Odin distinguished itself by cremating its dead. The reason for this was undoubtedly fear of the double. For while we have the delightful image of friends in their grave mounds talking to each other, we also have the image of the *draugr*, a vampire-like creature who left the mount to attack the living.

But there may have been an eschatological reason for this as well. One of the most ancient rites practised by the Zoroastrians is their funeral practices. Indeed, thoughts about how the dead should be handled are the hardest to change in any culture. In this there is a dog which must be brought up to the priest three times so the priest can touch it. The dog should have two spots, one above each eye (like an alsatian) and is called 'four-eyed'. Again, the opening of the wolf's mouth at ragnarok is suggested, for the dog is supposed to be a symbol of new life after struggling through the demonic forces that will try to claim the soul at the bridge of judgement. Ragnarok, too, of course, takes place next to a bridge.

Equally, the dead have their uses. Odin, himself, was a god of the dead. And he was quite willing to employ necromancy, to raise a *volva* (priestess/soothsayer) to get information out of her. As in all shamanism, the position of the dead was slightly ambiguous—useful and dangerous.

The rune itself is used in invoking the dead and, once they have been raised, of compelling them to answer questions put to them. It is connected with the chariot-god of the pagans, Thor, and with Mithras who also rode a chariot as a sun-sky god.

In addition to its connections with death, the rune is a symbol of change in the self. It is a symbol of new ideas, new ways of life, new ways of doing things. In all religions death is a symbol of coming renewal, and this rune partakes in that. In this way it is very similar to the Tarot card, Death.

Name: Ken	*Number*: 5
Sound: K	*Colour*: Yellow
Origin: The Greek letter Kappa, the Roman letter K	

Ken's magical image is of a torch, and is a symbol of magical power and of initiation. It is thus representative of power which is controlled, but has some measure of control itself. In this we should remember that the pagans used torchlight parades and bonfires to celebrate important events such as the vernal equinox and winter solstice. The torchlight was and is (the torchlight parades are still going) their symbol of Man having harnessed powers greater than his own.

It should be remembered that in myths, animals speak, have a sense of history, often wear clothes and use tools. But in no case do they use fire. This separated human from animal. In Mithrasism, for example, Mithras himself is accompanied with two lesser versions of himself, each of whom carries a torch. More, Mithras was born with a torch in his hand. In Zoroastrianism, fire is the purifying element. And in Germanic paganism, many initiations took place in caves. This allowed a combination of symbolism and experiences. The two main symbols which we can deduce are rebirth and the hidden light of the torches in the cave. This allowed the initiate to be put through a number of fearful incidents such as hanging over an edge, being buried alive, and being left in the dark until fear emerged and then being shown the great light which blinded by its power.

All these aspects are involved in the symbolism of this rune, which represents the harnessed power of light which emerges from the darkness. It is interesting that two other runes represent light; sighel, which is the sun; and doerg, which is the day. Only ken, though, is the harnessed power, and it is powerful image even in a highly technological society.

Name: Gyfu		*Number*: 6
Sound: hard G		*Colour*: Red
Origin: Hallristingnor carving shaped—X, the Greek letter xi		

This rune, which is also spelt gifu, represents a gift, an act of hospitality or piety, or a sacrifice to the gods. The nature of this sacrifice may be as little as a genuflection all the way to human sacrifice. To the Germanic pagans, living in a society when population was often small, hospitality might well be the difference between life and death to a traveller. Moreover, the rune reminds us of the dictum, 'a gift demands a gift'.

It should be mentioned that runic magic or divination requires a necessary balance of intent, actions, and results. They are an ecological form of magic. For example, it is always necessary to make a statement of intent or sacrifice for magical work, or to have all aspects of a question in mind before using the runes for divination.

It is possible that the symbolic content of the rune is its balance, being bilaterally symmetrical from all angles. That is, if you took mirror images of the rune by putting a mirror down the middle and turned it all the way around, you'd constantly have the whole image of gyfu. Only isa and doerg of the other runes share this trait. It should be remembered, though, that the runes are images of propagation of magical force (see next chapter) and this has much to do with their shape. So gyfu's shape may have been determined without an image in mind. However, it is notable that gyfu is a form of cross, which has always been a symbol of sacrifice in all its forms. It's a reminder to us of a truth the pagans knew but we try to forget; every decision which is of value encompasses a sacrifice.

Name: Wynn   *Number*: 8
Sound: W   *Colour*: Blue
Origin: Hallristingnor carving shaped—

The name 'wynn' means 'glory'. Odin was said to have carried a bundle of rods called 'glory wands' and to have practised rune magic with them. It was said he once met a snake and struck it with his wands, whereupon the snake fell into nine pieces. This seems to be a symbolic representation of flaying snakes, just as certain Zoroastrian priests did, on the belief that snakes were created by the supreme deity of evil, Ahriman.

It is probable that the story of the glory wands is part of a description of runic divination by Odin the shaman. Indeed, it was probably divination by the runes that helped their acceptance. It is a technique quickly used and adapted, but would always remind people of that particular cult.

The rune symbolizes power which is untapped, unharnessed. It is exuberant power, as opposed to ken's internal strength. Wynn is that divine power which, with a sudden thrust, forces human beings on to their destiny. The image is of a bundle of rods which are bound by a leather thong. Some of the thong hangs loose so it can be used as handle by a wandering shaman or berserk.

On a higher level, the rune is wisdom. The snake falling into nine pieces is significant, since nine was the most commonly-used number in pagan number-symbolism. Odin, remember, was the ninth creature created in the nine worlds. Nine has some lunar implications, but Luna was the masculine of the planets. The formula of wisdom is thus somewhat different. It is not glorious in the traditional sense, its glory comes from the fact that it is hard-won, and only by the difficulty of its achievement is it valued. This is implied in the wisdom of wynn, which is gained by the sacrifice of wisdom.

The above eight are Freyja's aettir, or family. Taken in order they provide a narrative of initiation in the form of a prayer. This is as follows.

> *Gathered for the sacrifice and feast, gifts are brought to*
> *Thy wild and divine power, which protects us from*
> *The frost demons who are the devourers of men.*
> *By thy inspiration*
> *We travel to that world of the dead and*
> *Are brought back.*
> *Thus we who sacrifice are initiated*
> *And return as the glorified ones of thee.*

As a discussion of initiation, the runes make the same points in less poetic terms. I am certain the reader can work these out with just a little effort, an effort which will be well-rewarded.

Name: Hoel   *Number:* 1
Sound: H   *Colour:* White
Origin: The Greek letter eta, the Roman letter H

This rune is a symbol of frost, ice, hail, and winter. The very things that were the weapons of the frost giants which were hinted at in the rune thorn. During winter months, the people of the north were largely trapped indoors. This often meant being stuck in the same room with people for months on end.

It was natural that a certain prankishness would emerge. In that sense the rune is a symbol of that lesser part in each of us that will come out with boredom. But it also implies the conquest of that, of being able to listen to the counsel of silence. This would explain why the rune of the trickster should be the rune to start Heimdall's aettir. Heimdall was partly the god of meditative silence and thus the one to overcome pranksterishness—i.e. the thief role of Loki, himself one of the giants.

The main thrust of the rune, though, is being bound, of frustration, of the unpleasant side of all of us. It should be remembered that in Germanic mythology, cross-breeding between giants, gods, and humans was quite common. There could thus be considered to be bit of god and giant in each of us. This rune is the symbol of the giant in us.

Name: Nyd	*Number:* 2
Sound: N	*Colour:* Blue
Origin: Hallristingnor carving shaped—†, the Latin Letters N or possibly H	

The rune nyd represents the power that makes someone do things that are impossible. It is an internal power, as opposed to ken, which is harnessed external power. It should also be compared to ur, which is unharnessed power. Nyd refers to that sudden rush of power that lets a person succeed in a crisis, or the sudden rush of destiny that lets all things fall into place.

Name: Isa	*Number:* 3
Sound: I	*Colour:* Black
Origin: The Greek letter iota	

This rune is a representation of the spear, which in its turn is one of the great weapons of Western magic. The spear has many forms, including the shepherd's crook and the staff. Again, the spear is not only the favoured weapon of Odin, but of Tiwaz. In his shamanistic form, Odin often carried a blackthorn staff.

In all these forms, the spear is a symbol of masculinity just as the cup is the symbol of femininity. The spear is a symbol of authority, and of power, of command and circumcision. In this context it carries some connotations of struggle and strife. It is taking challenges head on and meeting them, overcoming them. It is in many ways the symbol of the conqueror.

Name: Ger	*Number:* 4
Sound: Y	*Colour:* Brown
Origin: Hallristingnor carving of a swastika—	

The name of this rune, which has nothing to do with its phonetic use, refers to the esoteric meaning of the symbol—a year. The rune represents the annual period and particularly its harvest. It thus focuses concern where all the gnostic or mystery religions of the beginning of this age has their main focus; the harvest and planting of new crops as an analogy of death and rebirth. Mithrasism, too, had a focus like this in its use of bread and wine for a sacrament. The same concepts have been used in a number of religions including Judaism (Passover) and Christianity (Easter).

As such this rune is a pleasant symbol of community and festival. As such it lacks the tit-for-tat aspect of gyfu, and is a hospitality that is expansive and two-way. It has an element of plenty to it without indicating the wealth of either feoh or odel.

The rune is a representation of right action leading to right results as part of the natural order of things. In this it should be compared to nyd, which is a sudden burst of action while ger is long term activities which culminate in success. Again, it can be declared a sort of pole of hoel, which is wrong action leading to bad result. Ger is a rune of long term success through harmony with nature.

Name: Eoh	*Number*: 5
Sound: between E and I	*Colour*: Yellow
Origin: Hallristingnor carving shaped—	

The image presented may well be a fir tree, the yew, which was sacred to runecraft. As connifers, they bear male and female cones and hence are symbols of hermaphoditism and immortality. Being evergreens certainly adds to their symbolic importance, as is the fact that humans are barred from immortality by the fact that the needles are poisonous. In the same way, this is a symbol of the limits of life. We may see the stars, but only the gods may reach them, and it is too much to try and achieve the same thing ourselves.

In this the rune should be compared to gyfu. Gyfu is the embodiment of 'a gift demands a gift'. This rune is the embodiment of 'better not to pledge than to pledge overmuch'. This is the symbol of natural and rightful restriction which makes a good comparison with hoel, or unnatural restriction. It should also be compared with nyd. Nyd is the irresistible force, eoh is the immovable object.

Overall, it is a symbol, like ger before it, of our natural limits. But where ger is cycles, eoh is the static limits of the natural laws of the universe. It defines the areas in which we can move and act. But always it carries the connotation of great achievement that can be had eventually.

Name: Poerdh   *Number*: 6
Sound: P   *Colour*: Red
Origin: The Greek letter sigma?

Of all the runes, this one is the most mysterious. The meaning of the word *poerdh* has never been translated. Various authors, occult and academic, have given a number of theories about its origin and meaning. These include that it represents a dice cup and hence factors of chance and that it represents human sexuality. Neither theory fully convinced me, though at least the theory of the dice cup fits the shape of the rune.

Accepting that normal scholarship will be stuck until more material comes to light, I decided to astrally project into the rune. The rite I used is given later in this book. When I had the image, I confirmed by divination.

I found the image to be of a burial mound and its entrance. The rune is a symbol of that final boundary of human life, of death and a change in the state of being. It is not the same as rad, however, since poerdh encompasses a sense of loss, of finality, and to some extent of the price of failure. We should remember that life was hard in these times, and the death of relatives, children, spouse, or oneself was always near at hand. This is a symbol of the grave which is impenetrable.

Name: Eolh   *Number*: 7
Sound: Z   *Colour*: Purple
Origin: Hallristingnor carving shaped—

Used on its own, this rune is a sign of protection and can be used against the evil eye or other magical attack, trespassers, and the like. What its image is has been argued over for a long time. It has been suggested to be a representation of an elk's horn, the head of an elk about to butt (in which case compare with ur), and a splayed hand. Any or all of these may be correct. I would add to the list that it may represent a magician's wand, since in the pagan north wands were often splayed with two or three points at the business end. Where the symbolism of the wand came from, however, is another matter.

Defence was a major need in the pagan tribes. It was common that individuals or whole tribes were beset by opponents stronger than themselves. Any dominance they might achieve was certain to be short-lived. And the ability to guard all households at all times was just non-existent. Fear of raiding brigands or simply of fire always around. With such dangers, the magics of protection and turning aside enemies had to be plumbed. A single sign, quickly used, with a host of connotations to known and effective symbols of defence was the logical choice.

This rune also indirectly supports the interpretation of poerdh as death or some other sort of danger. Note that in the Germanic futhark, runes representing a danger are put next to runes representing protection or higher powers. Thorn is next to os, rad is next to ken, hoel is next to nyd. The same pattern seems to apply here. But if the rune is protection against such things as draugrs, there should also be rune against a more physical opponent. We find this rune a bit later.

For the moment, it should be remembered that eohl is a rune of protection against all hostile forces. Not necessarily evil forces, but simply hostile ones.

Name:	Sighel	*Number:*	8
Sound:	S	*Colour:*	Yellow
Origin:	Hallristingnor carvings of the sun, including the swastika and sunwheel, and the Roman letter S		

Sighel is a symbol of the sun, and hence is a symbol of salvation, spiritual protection, and the forces of light and order arranged against those of darkness and chaos. It is not the uncontrolled but controlling god-power of os, nor is it harnessed in the way of ken. Sighel is a transcendant power. Even when ragnarok was seen as the end of things, a new or reformed universe would survive, and Yggdrasil would spread its branches over a new age. This is the sort of power and salvation of sighel. It is the power of new life.

That completes Heimdall's aettir, or family. It does not have the simple narrative hook that Freyja's aettir enjoys, but does display a more complicated protocol or story-line. As in the narrative of the Tarot, there are two 'falls' or dangers to take into account.

> *Facing severe opposition and set-backs, he*
> *finds the strength beyond the human that enables him to*
> *establish the authority and banish the trouble, so that*
> *the crops can be harvested and the people fed.*
> *Attention then turns to the spiritual, which causes*
> *the powers of death to emerge, an internal enemy which manifests.*
> *A choice is made between physical and spiritual victory,*
> *And then the spiritual salvation is used which may or may*
> *not allow physical salvation.*

This, basically, is the plot of the Arthurian myth.

↑	*Name*: Tyr	*Number*: 1	
	Sound: T	*Colour*: Red	
	Origin: Hallristingnor carving shaped—↑		

Where eohl emphasizes protection from the magical but with elements of the physical, tyr is protection from physical danger with some element of protection from the magical. The name is the same as one of the variants of the god, Tiwaz, who was also called Tir. Just as Tiwaz was once the supreme deity of the Germanic pantheon and god of justice, war, and agriculture, the rune stands for victory, power, skill, protection from harm, and just success.

Tribal warriors would often paint this rune on their shields as a protection and to give them courage and valour in battle. It was also often carved or etched into the hilts or blades of pagan weapons.

The rune itself may be a representation of a spearhead, since the spear was Tiwaz's weapon as well as Odin's. It should also be noted that the one-handed god's image was carved into cave walls in the late Stone or early Bronze Age, so this is an ancient god with a long, continuous history. But, alternatively, the rune may be a symbol of the world pillar, which we know as the tree Yggdrasil. In the German assembly, the *thing* there was often a central pillar with wings at its apex (wings as an architectural device, not showing any similarity to bird or angel wings). This pillar represented the world pillar, and oaths could be taken on it. This practice of the sacred pillar was later adapted to the cult of Thor.

The rune tyr is a symbol of divine justice and the honour of war or duel. It is a symbol of strength of purpose, of the power of will, and of the drive to higher purpose. On a more immediate level, it is victory, courage, the power to attack. It is a weapon against enemies by making oneself stronger.

Name: Boerc	*Number*: 2
Sound: B	*Colour*: Blue
Origin: The Greek letter beta, the Roman letter B	

Boerc is a rune of healing, regeneration, and the atonement of past deeds. In this it ought to be compared to thorn, to which boerc is a kind of polar opposite. This rune is useful in aiding childbirth and in aiding the healing of minor diseases.

It is interesting that one of the pagan rites included flagellation with a bundle of birch twigs. This act had both magical and sexual connotations. Which makes it no surprise that this rune was also used for fertility. In parts of Scandinavia it is still the norm for someone coming out of a sauna to roll in the snow and then be beaten by birch twigs, which shows how hard some habits die.

Boerc is also a rune of atonement. It may have escaped some of today's social workers, but a person who has done wrong must be given a means of making up for that wrong. A fine or imprisonment may perhaps be less harsh than a task to do or even a public torture like flogging or pillory, but the latter erases the crime and binds society to a certain set of norms. In pagan minds, of course, wrongdoing and disease were normally connected.

Both society and the body were seen as having a 'normal' state of good health. Where this was lacking it was because there was some inhibitor at work. There was some pollution which had to be got rid of. A purging was needed, whether an emetic, blooding, prayers, public punishment, exorcism, or flagellation with birth twigs to make the body sweat all the harder from the sauna.

This rune is symbolic of all these attitudes. It is the negation of the pollution. It thus carries the tones of healing, fertility, and atonement.

Name: Ehwis   *Number*: 3
Sound: short E   *Colour*: White
Origin: The Greek letter mu, the Roman letter M, or possibly a symbol used by the pagan Spartans to worship Castor and Pollux.

Like several runes, ehwis is identified with a god, or in this case, gods. Tacitus describes a cult of twin gods among the Germanic tribes. These gods were called the Aclis, and the similarities to Castor and Pollux are as surprising today as they obviously were to Tacitus.

The Aclis were the sons of the sky god, probably but not definitely Tiwaz. They were excellent horsemen, and horses were central to the cult. Indeed, the word ehwis has the same derivation as 'horse'. And just as many Germanic royal houses traced their lineage back to Odin, so many traced their lineage back to an early pair of twins who shared their kingship. Heingist and Horsa, a pair of Saxon kings, are an example, and their names are 'horse' and 'stallion', respectively.

The rune may represent any one of a number of things, and in fact is very like a symbol used by the Spartans in their worship of Castor and Pollux. That symbol was two beams held together by a crossbeam, and has been explained as referring to a primitive bellows. It has also been suggested that this rune shows two horses' heads facing each other. Perhaps so.

Like Castor and Pollux, one of the Aclis seems to have killed the other. Also like the Greek gods, the Aclis' worship seems to have involved horse races. In the Aclis' case, the horsemen rode in pairs, joined together. This image may also be the meaning of the rune, a reference to the joined horsemen.

The rune is a symbol of the call for divine aid in times of trial and a gathering of the bonds of friendship. As in all rural communities, people may have been individualists, but that is always put aside in times of crisis. In this the rune should be compared to nyd, which is the individual calling on their own super-human resources. The emphasis of ehwis is the calling on external aid, much as ken is the harnessing of external power and os is the power which guides its own use. This is a conscious request and a conscious grant of external and often divine aid.

It is thus a useful charm against troubles, since it ensures aid when it is most needed. However, it is of no use to gain extra help when it is not essential. Like the other runes, ehwis has certain ecological and ethical limitations. It is a rune of defence, not of attack.

Name: Manu	*Number*: 4
Sound: 4	*Colour*: Purple
Origin: Hallristingnor carving shaped—, the Greek letter mu	

The word 'manu' and its attendant rune both represent man, either as an individual or the race as a whole. And in fact it includes the female of the species as well. It would be quite difficult to explain all the differences in the ideas of the role of Man in the universe. Paganism differs from Christianity and both differ from the modern scientific materialism most readers will be used to.

Essentially, it can be said that in materialism Man is central but irrelevant. In paganism Man is not central but is significant. That is, human beings in paganism have an essential role to play in that from them come the massed troops who will defend good from evil on the last of days. In materialism, it does not matter a whit to the universe if we nuke ourselves from the face of the planet, but at the same time everything that is known is measured from the yardstick of human beings. Things exist, not of their own right, but by their usefulness to us. This is one of the reasons all research today must justify itself on what it can do to allow us to transcend, manipulate, or profit from our environment. In pagan Germany and Greece, philosophy and poetry were allowed abstract study into intrinsic problems which had no direct influence on life itself.

There is a great deal more to the differences of view on the role of the human being than this (indeed, materialism is based on the view that there is no essential *human* role in the scope of things). However, exploring this fully would take a chapter or even a volume on its own. The pagan view of human beings, once understood, is enough to make the meaning of this rune clear. Without that understanding, no amount of explanation will make it clear. The pagan view of life is described throughout this work, and a practice of the runes will soon bring a deep understanding of that view of the world.

Name: Lagu   *Number:* 5
Sound: L   *Colour:* Green
Origin: Hallristingnor carving shaped—↑

Lagu represents water and the sea, and its image is of a wave breaking against the shore. Many of the Germanic peoples were seafarers, the Vikings being only one example of this. To any sea people, the sea is life but is also death. The sea is always shown as being greedy for ships, and the expression 'jaws of Aegir' carries this very connotation.

But water is also necessary to personal life. We die from lack of water long before we die of hunger. The early pagans were quite fond of beer, and the sea god Aegir was a brewer as well as a devourer of ships. Though it may seem disgusting to us, in early times beer was apparently made to ferment by spitting into the vat. This made the making and drinking of a batch of beer an admirable basis of an oath. Those who spat and drank were bound together, and this image appears in the myths we have. It appears in the myth of the mead of poetry and again in the *Lokasenna*.

Thus the rune has meanings of life-sustaining water, the oath of beer drinking or companionship, and death. It is basically a rune of transition from one state to another. From life to death, from individual to member of a group, and at birth, since the pagans splashed water on their newborns, too. It encompasses protection and danger, which is what every transition offers. It is a rune of oaths, treachery, and hope, and is thus quite logically placed next to the rune representing human beings. This is their role in life. Be born, live, join with others, and die in the name of their gods and against the chaos of the giants.

Name: Ing   *Number*: 6
Sound: Ng (as in thing)   *Colour*: Black
Origin: The Roman letter D

The rune means, simply, the people, and is often taken to mean the Danes, specifically. If that is correct, it may be a dim memory of Oller's overthrow of Odin. However, the name refers to an earth god that preceded Tiwaz, let alone Odin.

Symbolically, the rune refers to the importance of the community. Hence this rune can be used as a rune of fascination; to draw people or make them do what one wants. It can also be used to build the 'we' aspect of group, to establish mutual dedication and loyalty.

Name: Odel   *Number*: 7
Sound: O   *Colour*: Brown
Origin: ?

This rune refers to inherited property, goods, name, or traits. In this it is a complement to the rune ing. Perhaps their physical shapes' similarities are through design. Otherwise I can find no obvious origin to the shape of this rune, although a number of Hallristingnor carvings taken together suggest the shape of the rune, though none create the complete rune.

The pagans were much closer to their ancestors than we are today. The family name was a possession, and every child learned a sort of familial mythology in which their ancestors were extolled. In many places ancestors seem to have received worship. They were a part of the extended family of Germanic society.

This rune is used to call on ancestral powers, or to call up the doubles of the ancestors, themselves. It can be used to develop strengths and talents, including latent talents. It can be used to guard family fortunes and aid in building a dynasty. It is a symbol of the merchant class and especially the royalty among the Germanic peoples.

Name: Doerg   *Number*: 8
Sound: D   *Colour*: Yellow
Origin: Hallristingnor carving shaped—⋈

Doerg stands for day, the light of day, and the powers of light and goodness. In this it should be noted that among a number of the tribes there was worship of a sun chariot, models of which still exist and show a horse pulling a cart on top of which is a disc inlaid with gold representing the sun. The disc is set upright so people can see it, and the models are no doubt scale versions of full-size carts that were part of celebrations.

The rune has some similarities to ken and sighel, but is something of a promise of the final banishment of darkness in each of us. In this it shows some parallels to the myths of Mithras, who similarly promised a time and place of light for faithful followers.

Of its own, doerg is a good luck charm. It can be used to increase one's station in life. It can be used for advancement and development. On a higher plane, it can be used to stimulate spiritual growth and understanding. It can be used as an expression of universal love.

It is an appropriate rune with which to end the futhark.

That complete's Tiwaz's aettir, or family. Like the other two aettirs, it seems to have a collective meaning. Where the others are initiation and success through strife, this aettir seems to express an understanding of right life in a community which in turn is dedicated to its gods.

The gods offer cosmic justice and victory on earth,
immortality to come,
and aid in times of trouble. To gain this,
Man must fulfil his own duties in the scheme of things,
to pass through the doorways, to take the oath
to be one with the community around him,
one with his ancestors, to use inheritance and property,
on behalf of the forces of light and good.

This last point, of course, also implies obligations to those not with property. We thus return to the obligations of the wealthy at festivals, when they brought the cattle to be slaughtered. This leads us back to the aettir of Freyja.

To familiarize yourself with these runes, you should compare the meanings of various groups of runes. For example, compare all the brown runes or red runes, or all the runes with the value of three, and examine the similarities and differences in their meanings. When you've completed that exercise, you should have a thorough knowledge of every rune in the futhark. By then you will be more than ready to construct your own rune-sticks and/or rune-stones.

CHAPTER FOUR

Carving and Colouring the Runes

Whether you are practising rune magic or preparing your sticks or stones for divination, you will have to carve or colour your runes. Each of these runes has a specific order in which the strokes should be done.

For divination, you may use stones, sticks, or small cardboard pieces rather like small Tarot cards. What you use will often depend on very unmagical questions like your skill as an artist, what sort of gravel can be found near your home, and so on.

If you are going to use rune-stones, all you will need is twenty-four flat stones such as would be suitable for skipping across the water. These should all be as close to the same size and weight as possible. These are then painted in the appropriate colours.

For rune-sticks, the best woods to use are birch or yew, which are traditional to runecraft. However, you can use balsa wood or lemon wood if these prove easier for carving or burning. However, balsa wood is too light for most casting, though it is excellent if your intent is to burn the edifice after it is completed.

Rune-sticks can best be made in proportion to your body. For example, they can be the length from the tip of your middle finger to the heal of your palm, as wide as the middle finger, and half of the thickness at the tip. If you want longer sticks, make them the length from the tip of your middle finger to your elbow, the same width as before, and about the thickness of the first joint of your middle finger.

Carve or hot-wire burn into each stick one of the runes until you have a full set of rune-sticks. The rune should only be carved or burned into one side of the stick, the other three sides should remain blank.

This groove, from carving or burning, should then be painted over with the appropriate colour.

Traditionally runes had only one colour, red. This was obtained from ochre, a lead compound, or blood—animal or human. However, magic has advanced greatly in recent decades, indeed, since the 1880s, our technology explosion has in some ways kept pace with the technological explosion of electronics. For example, it has been discovered that each rune can be more effective when carved and coloured in a specific way. This includes the use of specific colours. This allows runes to be used, for example, as astral keys, a topic discussed later in this book.

It has puzzled traditional scholars why the runes are so angular. Of all the lettering systems of the world, only runes have no curves in them at all. This has been explained by suggesting that the runes were designed to be carved into wood, leather, or stone, and that curves would be difficult to execute. However, there were cryptographic representations of the runes that had curves in them, and many other signs had curves, such as the sunwheel. This is not the explanation.

However, the strokes make it easy to interpolate a line of prayer, poem, spell, or saying between work and would make it easier to define the rune in magical terms. Various lines of sayings could then reinforce the message of the rune. You will find in the instructions to follow that as you carve or colour a stroke of each rune, you must recite a line of a saying. Thus the direction of stroke and the lines of the saying each add to the esoteric meaning of each rune. So the method of carving and colouring the runes are bound together to be a small rite of runic magic, themselves. No special tools are needed, one simply uses whatever practical devices are needed to complete the task. The specific details of carving the runes are as follows.

Feoh is carved by starting at the upper right-hand side and carving the diagonal down and to the left, then the lower branch up and to the right. Then the vertical stroke is carved from bottom to top.

When coloured brown, the vertical stroke is coloured from bottom to top. Then the lower diagonal is carved down and to the left until it meets the vertical stroke. Then the upper diagonal is coloured from left to right. With each stroke, recite one line of the following.

Good things given,
good things received,
pleasure in life maintained.

Ur is carved from the upper left-hand corner, where the vertical and diagonal lines meet. It is carved along the diagonal stroke downwards and to the right, then down the right-hand vertical stroke. Then carve the left-hand vertical stroke from the upper left-hand corner straight down.

To colour the rune green start at the bottom of the left-hand vertical stroke. Colour the stroke upwards. Then colour the right-hand vertical stroke downwards. Finally, colour the diagonal stroke from left down to the right. The saying here is.

Danger and force,
I do face,
and win.

Thorn should be carved from the upper diagonal, which is carved down and to the right. Then the vertical stroke is carved downwards. Then the lower diagonal stroke is carved downwards and from right to left.

Like all three white runes, it can be coloured light grey if necessary. It is coloured by taking the vertical stroke straight down. Then colour the upper diagonal down and to the right, then the second diagonal from right to left and down. With each stroke, recite one line of the following.

Alone am I
when I face danger,
but never do I falter.

Carve os by starting with the vertical stroke and carving it downwards. Then carve the lower diagonal stroke from left to right, then the upper diagonal from right to left.

To colour it purple, start with the vertical stroke and colour it upwards. Then do the lower diagonal from left to right, and then the upper diagonal from right to left. With these strokes you say the following.

Divine power is called.
Divine grace is asked.
Call forth the gods.

Rad is a bit more difficult. Start at the centre. Carve the diagonal up and to the right. Next carve the vertical stroke downwards. Now start at the bottom right-hand side and carve the last stroke from the right up and to the left so you reach the top.
Now carve the last stroke from the right up and to the left so you reach the centre.

Rad is black, and the strokes are coloured in reverse order to their carving, both in order of strokes and direction. That is, start at the top of the rune and colour down and to the right. Then colour from the centre and to the right. Then colour the vertical stroke upwards. Next, colour the last stroke downwards and left along the diagonal, going from the right-hand side of the rune to its centre. For this rune recite the following.

For I shall take a journey,
on a horse no man can ride.
It has eight legs,
and it bears the dead.

Ken is rather easy to carve and colour. Start at the top and carve down and to the left, then down and to the right.
To colour it yellow, start at the joint where the two diagonals meet. Colour up and to the right, then down and to the right. For each stroke there's only one line to repeat, whether carving or colouring. You therefore will repeat the line four times. The line is:

I hold the light.

Gyfu, rather like ken, is easy to carve and colour. Start at the upper right and carve down and to the left. Then start at the lower right and carve the second diagonal up and to the left.
Gyfu is red. Start colouring from the upper right and colour down

and to the left. Then start at the upper left and colour down and to the right.

In this case, though, you have to recite different lines when carving and colouring. When carving, recite the following.

A gift
demands a gift.

When colouring say,

As I demand,
so I provide.

To carve wynn start from the top of the vertical stroke and carve straight down. Then carve the upper diagonal down and to the right, and finally the lower diagonal down and to the left so the stroke comes back to meet the pillar again.

To colour it blue, start at the very top and colour the diagonal down and right. Then colour the lower diagonal down and left, back to the vertical which has not been coloured in. The vertical is coloured last, and this is coloured from bottom up.

When carving or colouring, recite the following.

The glories are many
if you follow the path
unto its end.

Hoel is carved starting with the right-hand stroke, which is carved straight from top to bottom. Then the diagonal is carved up and to the left. Finally, carve the left-hand vertical upwards.

To colour it white (or grey) start with the diagonal and colour it down and to the right. Then colour the left-hand vertical from bottom up and then the right-hand stroke from bottom to top. For this rune, the following is said.

Ice and hail
are my enemies
without fail.

Nyd is carved by starting with the vertical stroke and carving that straight down. Then the diagonal is carved down from left to right.

Colouring is done in the same direction but with the strokes in reverse order. That is, the diagonal stroke is coloured downwards and to the right, and then the vertical stroke is coloured from top to bottom. Nyd is blue, like wynn. Like gyfu, you recite different lines when carving and colouring. For carving the lines are as follows.

What I need,
I achieve.

When colouring, recite.

I've got the power,
I achieve.

Isa is about as easy a rune as you can hope for. Carve it from bottom up; colour it black from top down. In either case recite:

My spear flies true.

To carve ger, start at the top of the upper vertical stroke, at the very top of the rune, and carve down. Then carve the lower vertical down. Then carve the diagonal stroke up and to the right.

Colouring it brown, do the diagonal stroke from left to right, then the right-hand vertical stroke down. Finally, colour the left-hand or upper vertical stroke from where it joins the diagonal to the top of the rune. The lines here are as follows.

Harvest time and planting time
the crop is cared for
and made to grow.

Eoh, the yew tree, is carved from the top. First the upper diagonal is carved down and to the right. Then the vertical is carved downwards, and then the lower diagonal is carved down and to the right so it meets the base of the rune.

To colour it, start with the lower diagonal and colour this up and to the left. Then colour the vertical stroke upwards. Lastly, colour the upper diagonal down and to the right. In this case, the rune is green and this is what you recite.

Though poisonous the fruit,
immortal is the promise
of the sacred tree.

To carve poerdh, start by carving the vertical stroke straight from top to bottom. Then, from that bottom point, the lower and inner diagonal is carved up and to the right. Then the outer upper diagonal is carved upwards and to the right, which will leave it sort of hanging from nothing for a moment. Next, the outer lower diagonal is carved down and to the right. Finally, the upper, inner diagonal is carved down and to the right so it connects the diagonal that's been hanging in the air.

The rune is coloured red. Start at the upper right-hand point of the outer and upper diagonal. This is coloured inwards and downwards, heading to the left. Follow the next diagonal up and to the left, which brings you to the (uncoloured) vertical stroke. The vertical stroke is now coloured straight down. This will give you something that looks a bit like a flagpole and a flag. Next, colour the lower inner diagonal up and to the right. Then colour the outer lower diagonal down and to the right. In other words, when colouring the rune you follow it straight around.

When carving or colouring, do not recite the words out loud but think them to yourself.

Death
is a journey
and a change
that always leads
to new life.

When carving Eohl, start by carving the vertical stroke straight down. Then carve the left diagonal up and to the left, and then the right diagonal up and to the right.

When colouring it purple, colour the vertical stroke straight up, then the right diagonal down and to the left. Then colour the left diagonal down and to the right. When carving or colouring, you must recite the following:

By my sword,
and by my magic
I am defended.

Sighel is the only rune where the strokes are coloured and carved in the same order and direction. Starting from the top of the rune, go down and to the left, up and to the right, then down and to the left. The rune is yellow, and the lines are:

Sun and wind,
light of day
will perfect the world again.

Tyr is carved from the spearpoint. Start by carving the left-hand diagonal down and to the left. Then carve the vertical stroke downwards. Finally, carve the second diagonal down and to the right.

Tir should be coloured red, which is logical for a rune which represents a god of war. Start by colouring the vertical stroke straight down. Then colour the left-hand diagonal down and to the left. Then colour the right-hand diagonal down and to the right. When carving or colouring, recite the following.

Vault of the sky,
justice and power,
I defend thee.

Carving boerc, start with the uppermost diagonal and carve down and to the right. Then carve the third diagonal from the top (the one second from the bottom) from where it meets the centre of the vertical stroke; carve it down and to the right. Next, carve that vertical stroke upwards. This should now give you something looking a little like the rune os. Next, carve the lowermost diagonal up from the base of the vertical. Then lastly the diagonal from the centre of the vertical stroke. This will be carved up and to the right, and completes the rune.

Boerc is blue, and to colour it, start by doing the vertical stroke from bottom to top. Then colour the lowermost diagonal up and to the right. Then colour the second lowermost diagonal, the one second from the top, down and to the right. Then colour the last and uppermost diagonal down and to the right. In this way you've coloured the diagonals from bottom to top.

When carving this rune, you recite nothing. Only when colouring do you recite anything, and that is:

Life eternal,
fertility,
freedom and joy,
are provided
to initiates.

Ehwis: carve the left diagonal down and to the right first, then the right diagonal up and to the right. Then carve the left vertical straight down, then the right vertical straight down.

To colour ehwis white or grey, colour the right-hand vertical straight up, then the left-hand vertical straight down. Then colour the right diagonal from right to left downwards, then the left diagonal from left to right, also going downwards. For carving and colouring, the following is recited.

Far and wide
the brothers roam
to aid those
who seek their help.

To carve manu, carve the vertical strokes first. Start with the left one, then the right one. Both are carved from bottom to top. Then carve the diagonal strokes, first downwards and to the right, then downwards from right to left.

The rune is purple and to colour it colour the diagonals first. Colour down and to the right, then down and to the left. Next do the vertical strokes, colouring the left one upwards and the right one downwards.

When carving, recite one line for each stroke, choosing whichever first line you feel more comfortable with.

With my god/s or *With my os/en*
by my sword
with my harvest,
I live.

When colouring, the following are the lines to recite.

from birth
to grave,

I live by justice,
and by my oath.

Lagu is carved by cutting the vertical stroke downwards, then the diagonal stroke downwards and to the right.

When colouring it green, first the vertical stroke is coloured upwards, then the diagonal is coloured downwards and to the right. This time, recite.

Life grows,
Life goes on.

Ing is carved by cutting the two right-hand strokes first. Start at the top and carve downwards and to the right, then downwards and to the left. Then carve the two left-hand strokes, carving the upper diagonal down and to the left, then the lower stroke down and to the right.

When colouring the rune, colour the left-hand side first. Colour the top left-hand diagonal down and to the left, then the lower diagonal down and to the right. Then colour the two right-hand diagonals the same way. Colour the top one down and to the right, then the lower one down and to the left. The rune is coloured black.

When carving or colouring, the following should be said.

My people
who support me,
I shall support
by right action.

To carve odel, start with the lowermost left-hand point and carve the diagonal up and to the right. Then cross over to the joint on the left-hand side and carve the lower diagonal down and to the right. You should now have an 'x' rather like gyfu. Next, go to the topmost point and carve the upper diagonal down and to the right. Then carve the last diagonal down and to the left.

To colour the rune brown, start at that same lowermost left-hand point and colour the diagonal up and to the right, then turn the joint and colour the upper diagonal up and to the left so you reach the apex of the rune. Then, from the lowermost right-hand point, colour the diagonal up and to the left, then colour the upper diagonal up and to the right to complete the rune. Recite:

My ancestors,
my self, (sic)
my children,
the rope is unbroken.

Doerg is carved by starting with the left vertical stroke. Carve this downwards. Then carve the diagonal up and to the right, followed by the right-hand vertical stroke being carved downwards. Finally, the second diagonal is carved down and to the right.

To colour it, start at the top left and colour the vertical downwards. Then colour the right vertical stroke downwards. Next, from the top left of the left vertical stroke, colour the diagonal down and to the right. Then colour the second diagonal upwards and to the right. This rune is yellow.

Of all the runes, only this one is carved and coloured with no recitation. Total silence of the mind is to be kept at all times, so no words should form in the mind at all.

By these methods of carving and colouring the runes, a basic magical charge should be instilled in each one before you begin. This can be before beginning to prepare a magical talisman, or it can be before beginning divination. It is to the process of divination we shall be turning next.

Before embarking on a serious study of divination by the runes, you should already have made for yourself a set of runes on stones, sticks, or cards. If you are making cards, simply colour on the runes, this will still give you good effect. And now, onwards.

CHAPTER FIVE

Divination

Almost every method of divination is a philosophy about the world presented as a series of symbols which in turn provide answers to questions by a method or system of probability. The only systems that fall outside this rule are such fortune-telling devices as tea-leaf reading and certain dionysian techniques such as trances, astral projection, and automatic writing. And that fact is fundamental enough to be definitive, although no other book on divination has ever mentioned it, before.

This is not a work on the mathematics of divination, so it would be impossible to explore the differences between the coins that generate the *I Ching* hexagrams, the cards that generate the Tarot spreads, and the casting by lots that provide answers for the runes. Suffice to mention here that the nett effect of these differences is that each method is better suited to answer certain sorts of questions than the others. When dealing with the runes you have to be careful about the type of question you form and you have to keep the whole picture in your mind when asking for an answer from the runes.

Forming a Question

There are three basic rules to use when forming a question for the runes.

First, keep the question simple. Don't ask questions that require subclauses or parenthetical asides. Never ask two questions at once. If a problem is too big to ask in one question, think again. The 'if-I-do-this-and-I-do-that-what-will-happen-then?' sort of question does not work.

Second, make certain the question is specific. Avoid all idioms and always be certain of the four basic elements of a question:

What do you want to know?
Whom do you wish to know it about?
In what **time frame** is the question set?
Where is the question set?

Third, be direct. The question should go to the heart of the matter without taking detours. This is part-and-parcel with not using euphemisms, but also points out that asking a question in a tentative way will get you just as tentative an answer.

With the runes you can fit every question into one of three categories and one of three forms. The categories are based on the aettirs of the futhark, and the forms are based on the eight colours of the runes. The three categories are:

Love, life, and happiness, which relate to the aettir of Freyja.
Achievement, money, power, victory, and success, in which case it relates to Heimdall's aettir.
Intellect, understanding, and spiritual achievement, which relate to Tiwaz's aettir.

The eight forms a question can take are as follows.

What sacrifice will I have to make to. . .? What dangers will face me if I. . .? Then the rune will be red.

What money will I need/gain in relation to. . .? What will others say about. . .? What are the outer appearances of. . .? Then the rune will be brown.

What joys are due. . .? What aid is available/will come to. . .? Is this action/intent just? What is the inner nature of. . .? Then the rune is yellow.

Is the attempt to. . .wise? What creativity is involved in. . .? What forces outside myself/my conscious control are at work in. . .? In these cases the rune shall be green.

At what level of competance? Am I ready to. . .? Is it possible to . .? Then the rune shall be blue.

Is it right to __? Am I able to. . .? Will _____ allow the balance of things to continue without stress? In these cases the rune is purple.

What opposes. . .? What wrongs are weighing on. . .? What karmic debts are owed by. . .? Then the rune is white.

What constrains. . .? What keeps _____ from right action? What advice should be sought/given? Then the rune is black.

Take a simple example. Suppose the question is, 'Will I get wealthy in the ____ calendar year?' This question falls under category two, which is Heimdall's aettir. It is in form two, which means it should be brown. When we look for the brown rune in Heimdall's aettir we find it is ger, the harvest.

If the form of the question had been, 'What will I have to do to become wealthy in the ____ calendar year?', we would have had the first form of Heimdall's aettir, and would have looked for a red rune. This would have been poerdh, the funeral mound.

Turn the question again. 'Would I be happy if I became wealthy in the ____ calendar year?' The question is now in Freyja's aettir, and we're looking for the yellow rune for 'what joys are due. . .?' The rune is ken, the torch.

And so on. It only takes a little practice to become quite skilled in forming a question and determining a significator from the form of the question. Our next step is to learn the meaning of the individual runes, themselves.

Interpreting the Runes

Whether cast or laid, a rune will come down in one of four positions; face up upright, face up reserved, face down upright, face down reversed. The only exceptions are runes that are the same upright and reversed, like gyfu. Nevertheless, there are still some eighty divinatory meanings to the runes, as opposed to sixty-four *I Ching* hexagrams and 156 Tarot meanings (78 cards that can be upright or reversed). The divinatory meaning of the runes are as follows.

ᚠ Feoh

Face up upright: Good fortune, fertility, increase in property and success in endeavours.

Face up reversed: Infertility, bad luck, lack of control, especially lack of financial control, wastefulness.

Face down upright: To complete things you must take into account secret forces in yourself and others. The powers of creativity cannot be commanded, they must be coaxed. Forces out of control.

Face down reversed: Favourable forces are at work, but in secret. Can often indicate a blessing in disguise. May also indicate a chance to capitalize on events if one is willing to retreat temporarily. Sometimes when obstacles are insurmountable, we have to go south to go north.

Ur

Face up upright: Exuberance, inspiration, a suggestion you demand your place in the sun. Shows the conquest of one's lower nature. A strong will. It indicates someone in control of their internal world and who now seeks to control the world about them, too.

Face up reversed: Harshness, cruelty, and brutality. A person who cannot accept differences of opinion. Immaturity of mind leads to an attempt to dominate. It also shows cruelty is a mask for insecurity. A dictator whose reign is probably approaching its end.

Face down upright: Danger surrounds you. Shows unsettled conditions and forces at work averse to you. This is not an image of hostile forces or enemies, but impersonal events and forces which will still work in a way that, from your position, will be keeping you from your goals. It shows rough times ahead, and may indicate a test of your fortitude on the way.

Face down reversed: Impotence, lack of strength, energy, or ability to move. A barrenness of ideas has descended, a doldrums in which any attempt at movement has been frustrated. You must face a fallow time before you can again reap rewards. This is an inevitable period of pause and you have to accept it and even learn how to use it.

Thorn

Face up upright: A journey in the mind or body. A change of opinion often equals a change of scene, and both are necessary in life. An updating of thoughts and a reappraisal of things may be in order. Remember that when you travel, you have to weigh carefully what you will bring with you and what you will leave behind. Travel in your mind and leave behind the mental baggage you no longer need.

Face up reversed: Stagnation, refusal to face facts and to change with changing situations. May also mean a message of bad news, but one that is likely to be self-imposed. A warning that you must reassess your life and not assume that things will continue on as they have.

Face down upright: Instability and change. Can also mean things are not what they seem. This can be the image of the freed Loki, a trickster who can cause damage and danger if not watched. Look around carefully, there is possibly someone near you who, if not absolutely malicious is certainly mischievous enough to cause you some real harm.

Face down reversed: False promises, deceipt. A warning to take care about what is being said around you. It can mean you are being lied to, that your own lies will trip you up, or that lies are being told about you. Remember that in Zoroastrian mythology, people were followers of the truth or followers of the lie, and the lie was an objective pollution. This position of the rune warns you that such a pollution is about. It must be dealt with or there will be danger of collapse.

ᚩ **Os**

Face up right: Divine power, usually beneficent to you. This power may be in an impersonal form, or may be disguised through a human being. So this rune also suggests that you listen to the advice of someone older than you. It is also a recommendation of the value of prayer and propitiation of the gods. Events are now dominated by forces which are outside your control, but are not quite the same as the forces of destiny. Be aware of them, be aware of how to ride those forces, but understand you will never divert them to your own use.

Face up reversed: Misjudgement. The outcome will be ignominy and disaster if you don't change the course of your actions. Remember that what worked yesterday might not work today, you have to adapt and change to meet new situations.

Face down upright: The strength of will to explore new realms. The self has the power to change the self. Shows the ability to take risks and face dangers with the knowledge that though not all is known, much more than is known can be intuited. Shows successful risk-taking, and is generally a good omen for the starting of enterprises.

Face down reversed: Destruction and calamity. Problems that you have brought upon yourself. The destruction of barriers put up in oneself and which should have been torn down long ago. Depression, loss of income, possibly the loss of a loved one by death or break-up.

ᛁ Rad

Face up upright: Exploration into non-mundane realms of being, whether the realm of the dead or the higher planes of consciousness. The revelation of hidden things by divination, intuition, deduction or confession. Usually, the penetration to these other realms or through pretences is a positive attribute, but does denote a need to control matters to be able to get the information. When Odin spoke to a dead volva (priestess) to learn what Baldur's dreams meant, he had to force her shade to answer each round of questions. Similar strictures are applied in this case, and where the fate is too strong, it can be similarly fruitless to try to avert the events.

Face up reversed: A crisis of faith, a challenge to the way things are seen. The intuition can win through, logic and mundane knowledge cannot. Learn to trust your instincts, they have been honed over millenia of evolution while your personal knowledge has been developed over your lifetime.

Face down upright: The law is for all, it binds the high and the low, the rich and the poor. The law must be iron; unbreakable, secure, impersonal. It also indicates sacrifice, and that results never come without making a sacrifice. 'A gift demands a gift', and in the same way effort is necessary to succeed at anything worthwhile. 'There ain't no free lunch' is a more recent way of saying it. Be prepared to receive in proportion of what you put into life, a project, or an investment.

Face down reversed: Greed, cruelty, evil, and an alignment with the chaotic forces. This is the position of Hel and Loki, who were beings of the dead who came to oppose the gods. It is also the position of Nighogg, who tore apart the people who died in an unpurified state. It shows wrong action, false plans, and attempts to gain what does not rightfully belong to one.

Ken

Face up right: Energy, enthusiasm, optimism, learning. It is an indication of good fortune which is earned. Plans are being laid which are sound and the sense of timing is right. Things will go your way. It indicates success and triumph. You can overcome the obstacles in your path, and you can achieve your goals in life if you are just willing to reach for them.

Face up reversed: Uncertainty and shyness which is self-imposed. It is an indication you are discounting your own talents and abilities, and should be more forthcoming. It is an assurance that the raw abilities you need are there, even if they aren't yet brought to fulfilment by practice. You should be more forthcoming and remember that if you're willing to do something, you're already that much closer to having done it.

Face down upright: A lack of will-power. Dissipation of talent, money, or inheritance. A tendency to squander what has been gained. Liscentiousness and profligacy. Get a hold on yourself, you are in danger of falling under the influences of outside forces or of fetishes. Beware of alcoholism.

Face down reversed: A self-destructive streak that will snatch defeat from the jaws of victory at whatever price. Something in the self that must be overcome before any further progress can be made on the spiritual path. A warning to pull back from activity in order to think things through more clearly.

Gyfu

Face up: A sign of hospitality and friendship, of joy and celebration. It indicates liberality, compassion, and generosity of spirit. It can also indicate a romance is on the horizon.

Face down: Satiation, indolence, laziness, and a lack of effort. The physical senses have been drowned. Fatigue will now set in. May indicate an illness coming, but not a serious one.

Wynn

Face up upright: Happiness, success, the fruitful conclusion of an endeavour. Indicates a person who is deserving of their success and rewards. Proper payment for effort extended.

Face up reversed: Folly and foolishness. False assumptions lead to false conclusions no matter how faultless the logic. Indicates a reckless and impulsive attitude that acts first and fast, and then repents at leisure.

Face down upright: Material success and comfort. Wealth. Popularity. The chance of physical pleasures including an affair or similar encounter. Being a pagan divinatory system, this description contains no 'sting-in-the-tail' aspect. So long as the physical is enjoyed in its place, its enjoyment is seen as good.

Face down reversed: A warning of hidden dangers and traps. It may not indicate deceit so much as something you are overlooking. Sit back a bit and think things through again. What have you forgotten about? What enemies have you assumed are unimportant who may not be?

ᚺ   Hoel

Face up: Struggle and effort are needed. Victory can still be won, but only at a cost. True effort will be needed to get through to victory or even a draw. Conflict that cannot be avoided. Can also mean the destruction of the obsolete, the removal of the irrelevant.

Face down: Loss, abandonment, defeat. May indicate a project now under way is in trouble because of a lack of sustained effort. You are probably going to suffer material hardship and defeat, and the root cause will be yourself. May also show a blessing in disguise, for your defeat, however humiliating, is necessary for you to win through in a later battle.

ᚾ   Nyd

Face up: Great opportunities are at hand. Success cannot be bounded. Victory, triumph, and great messages are presaged by this rune. The opportunities must be grasped, but if they are, they will lead to wealth, achievement, and power.

Face down: You will face a powerful opponent who can be defeated. Do not listen to doomsayers or to the false counsel of others. You have reserves of strength that you have not yet touched. With patient planning, you can overcome your problems by cutting bits of the problem away and dealing with that bit by giving it your whole attention, then moving on to the next bit.

| Isa

Face up: Divine justice and authority in the face of strife and trouble. Whatever else others may do to you, they can never take away your honour. You will always have the chance to get back up and fight again with greater strength. Justice is invincible, and we need only act in accord with that to win through.

Face down: News and messages. An indication that negotiation will achieve more than conflict. May also indicate you are making enemies where there were none before. Be careful how you present yourself, a friend can be a reserve of help in times of trouble. There was a saying among the Germanic pagans, 'The road to a friend's house is always straight, even through thick forest'. This position also reminds us that to have a friend you must be a friend.

↳ Ger

Face up: The time of harvest; this position indicates joy, happiness, and communal spirit. It shows good times and a just reward for hard work is just around the corner. It can be a disquietening sign for anyone who's been coasting through life, just as there can be bad harvests, but this is not the major thrust of the symbol. It is basically a rune of celebration and joy. It shows successful endeavours having been undertaken.

Face down: A pause between two periods of intense activity or hard work. This is a time for sowing, not for reaping. If you have started a business or similar enterprise, this is not the time to take out, but to continue to build up. Burdens will ease, giving you more time, but that is about as much of an improvement as you can expect.

∫ Eoh

Face up: The greatest secrets, the most powerful worlds, and the greatest movements in history could all be summed in the span of a man's hand. Neither overreach yourself nor seek too little. Though you have your limits don't think too shallowly of them. There are opportunities for growth and intuition. Seize them.

Face down: Emotional instability, chicanery. You are deluding yourself more than you are deluding others. You must learn about yourself and to master yourself if you are ever to be successful in life. Begin a journey of inner exploration immediately.

⼁ Poerdh

Face up upright: Indicates a time of crisis, which is not only a time of emergency and the need for immediate action, but also a judgement. This is a time of many choices being open to you, but what you choose now will affect your life for a long time to come. You must choose wisely, and in this world, that means this rune is most often a danger sign.

Face up reversed: Stagnation, infertility, decay. May indicate a death in the family. A rune of the funeral mound in its most dislikeable aspect.

Face down upright: Defeat, chaos, dissipation. A warning to always remember that you may die at any moment. Since death was close to the Germanic pagans, they could let it be their advisor. It told them what was essential and what was not. This is what you must realize. There are things that aren't worth fighting for because they aren't strategic to the summing up of your life.

Face down reversed: Chaos, defeat, destruction. Some things cannot be avoided, and to try to avoid them is to cause even greater hardship for yourself and others. Submit yourself to your fate and to the right workings of the universe. In the end you have put yourself in an untenable position, let it collapse and then start to build anew.

⼂ Eohl

Face up upright: Health, pleasure, and attainment. An unassailable position of power, achievement, and success. It indicates the warding off of enemies. This is being on top of the mountain where you can really enjoy yourself.

Face up reversed: A reminder to employ charity when considering the plights of others. Even woes which are self-inflicted may need the help of others if they are to be overcome. You should be kinder when considering others, and put yourself in their shoes once in a while.

Face down upright: Dishonesty. Wealth gained by improper and dishonest means. This may be a warning to change your behaviour, but is more likely to be a warning that someone else is cheating you. Let the buyer beware. A suggestion to go over all contracts and agreements carefully, and generally to look before you leap.

Face down reversed: You have let your defences down too much. Like a country that has no army, you have to rebuild in the face of threat from outside. Now is the time to build up your savings and to pay off debts. This is a warning of bad times which may be impartial (like a depression) or personal (someone will put pressure on you at work). You have got to start building up now. Also suggests you should have a thicker hide against slander. Build your physical health so you won't become ill or exhausted during the stressful times ahead of you. And marshal your allies.

⚡ Sighel

Face up: A just reward received, achievement. Abilities coming to the fore. Good fortune and beneficence. An upturn in luck. This is a general symbol for good luck and happiness.

Face down: Shows you are trying to balance too many things at once. You can only do so much at a time. Can also mean imbalanced forces, relying too heavily on one aspect of things. Pull back from some activities so there is time, money, and energy to devote yourself well to those things which are left.

↑ Tyr

Face up upright: Justice, arbitration, the setting or rules and codes of conduct. This rune emphasizes the need to be fair and equitable in all your dealings. It also means you have to pull your own weight, so that you neither let others get away with too much nor take anything from them. It is also a reminder you have to keep up with your part of the bargain.

Face up reversed: Duel, struggle. You are going to have to fight for your honour and good name. Others will demand that you prove yourself, you cannot demand their respect without it. Learn to stand on your own two feet.

Face down upright: Temptation. The danger of a moral lapse. A reminder that what is too good to be true is probably false. When you have laid a plan, it is often better to stick to that plan in the face of a chance at a fast buck rather than make the grab. Slow development is not spectacular, but it is also likely to be far more secure and long-lasting. Stick to what you know is right and moral, however tempting other offers may seem.

Face down reversed: Idealism and struggle, a chance to offer yourself to a cause. It is only recently in history that people have had the notion they can live for themselves and only themselves. The Germanic pagans never had that notion. They knew they had to live with their tribe and their gods. This is a reminder that to live a full life you need not only daily bread, but a *worthwhile* cause to live for. That does not mean giving a guru a lot of money, it does mean a cause with honour.

▷ Boerc

Face up upright: Abundance and plenty, possibly a marriage or romance. It shows a time of emotional stability and happiness. It may indicate a port in a storm, a chance to get away from troubles rather than try to fight them out.

Face up reversed: Indicates a change in the sphere of emotional ties, a severing of links that have outlived their usefulness. You will be undergoing a major change in life, with new attitudes, friends, and activities. The old and obsolete must go, must be ruthlessly banished, for only then can new growth occur.

Face down upright: You are facing a series of choices, and are going to have to face a bit of a rough time until you make the right choice or choices. In the main, the choices are between convention and what you really want, but you have to make that choice when the crunch comes for anything to come of your resolve.

Face down reversed: Self delusion, castles in the air, fantasy. You are not being realistic in your goals or your actions. A suggestion that whatever promise has been made cannot be and will not be kept.

⋀ Ehwis

Face up upright: Strength, courage, tenacity, and perseverance are all being shown. Shows the ability to complete a task no matter what, and to take on troubles and beat them one-by-one.

Face up reversed: A warning against carrying grudges. Shows a moody, sullen, sulky disposition. A reminder to forgive and to forget.

Face down upright: Aid from other quarters is coming. Seek outside support if the task is a large one. No matter how bleak things are now, there is a dawn coming, and help can be found.

Face down reversed: Ambition, adventure, and enterprise. It shows a good mental attitude, a willingness to give it a go. However, if badly aspected it can indicate a headstrong nature, someone who can't see the wood for the trees.

ᛗ Manu

Face up upright: In this position the rune usually indicates the querent, and takes its character from the runes around it. It can also indicate the need for a careful balancing of the elements. Things when in the right mixture and the right proportion get the right results.

Face up reversed: A warning not to be inflexible. Vary your method of attack from time to time. This does not indicate a change in goals or even in strategy, but in tactics. Think things through again and figure out another path to your goal.

Face down upright: The chance of self-betterment. Transmutation of things from worse to better. The suggestion of a great opportunity coming up in the near future which you should grab with both hands.

Face down reversed: The lust for power. Greed and avarice. A warning that your actions and intentions are wrong, and that you will pay for this sooner or later. When the world seems horrible, you'd do better to reform yourself than to try to reform the world.

ᛚ Lagu

Face up upright: Sustenance, nourishment, either at the primal level or more generally. In the modern world it tends to mean ability, happiness, a change of luck for the better. Positive destiny, rewards.

Face up reversed: A change of consciousness, an alteration of ideas through growth. Internal changes in the emotional and spiritual spheres. Evolution.

Face down upright: A change in luck for the worse. The possibility of being sucked down with troubles. May indicate madness or other extreme distress. Dissipation. May indicate unbridled sexual urge. Satiation.

Face down reversed: Turning to the past, but may be for lessons, comfort, or in living in the past. Which of the three possibilities it is will depend on what runes lie near it. What action is suggested will depend on that.

◇ **Ing**

Face up upright: Wisdom and advice from others. The gathering of friends. The laying of foundations that will last long. A good time in a person's life. The approval of others.

Face up reversed: Teaching others, giving good advice. May indicate writing or publishing in some manner, since the idea of communication is certainly involved. Indicates you have knowledge and skills that others prize highly, and which you should share with others.

Face down upright: Worldly ambition for wealth, control, conquest, or self-control. Shows an iron will backing up a particular dream which may be good or evil. Shows a willingness to sacrifice in order to get that goal, but also shows a willingness to sacrifice all out of proportion to the value of the goal itself. Naturally, there's a strong element of stubbornness and myopia attached to this position of the rune.

Face down reversed: Criminal intent! Shows the righteous disapproval of the community. Somebody is treading on thin ice and should remember that there are higher forces that can and do exact revenge. It is also a reminder that the end doesn't justify the means, and you can't take unhonourable action because the enemy will do the same. You don't break the rules because 'they will sooner or later'.

◇ **Odel**

Face up upright: This rune may indicate a good marriage or family inheritance, but it generally signifies family ties, traditions, and filial duties. The family was very important to the tribes, and that meant more than the nuclear family we've come to know. Uncles, aunts, and cousins all had their duties as well. No matter what else, your family is your family, and acceptance of them means acceptance of certain obligations towards them. This rune reminds you of those duties and normally indicates they are not being fulfilled.

Face up reversed: Help is available from others. Shows the querent has been isolated for some time, but now has others to whom he or she can turn. A suggestion to turn to others who may have the answer you are looking for.

Face down upright: The overcentralization of power. There is a disbalance of things, here. Indicates that there is no give-and-take in a relationship. Normally also indicates a lack of trust. A suggestion that you think things over and see where everything is going wrong. Assert your rights (especially within the family) and allow others their rights. Everyone must have some space that is wholly and exclusively their own.

Face down reversed: Wealth, money, an inflow of capital. An indication that you will soon be in control of things. Power in a monetary sense is now within your grasp.

⋈ Doerg

Face up: A culmination of matters. A successful conclusion to things, whether negotiation, an enterprise, or an education. Spiritually, indicates attainment and the transmutation of consciousness to a higher plane. It is successful initiation and the spirit taking control of daily affairs. This rune is the power of the sun, which was life-giving day, and so partakes of the power of the various sun-kings such as Jesus and Mithras. It is the power of renewal and in divination it shows the growth of that power. It is success in all its forms.

Face down: The same power, but lately. Indicates new developments are forthcoming. The present position is not the end of things. Usually means you have gone into the field too early and should retire for further thought, preparation, and training. Many also indicate you would benefit from a period of abstinence or meditation.

Divination

In Tacitus' work, *Germania*, a method of divination by the runes is described. Thinking of the question, the rune-master would choose three strips of bark from a bag. On those strips of bark were written runes, and from the runes the diviner would learn the answer. Naturally, there was a strip of bark for each of the runes of the futhark in the bag, and the diviner had a white cloth which was spread before each consultation, but the core of the method we're looking at is the method of choice. Even though Tacitus was writing in the first century AD, the runes are still chosen in much the same way, depending on what you have carved and/or coloured them on.

Basically, there are two methods of choosing the runes for your divination. They can be mixed and then tossed as a lot, or shuffled or mixed and chosen like Tarot cards. Since the latter method will be more familiar to most readers, we'll concentrate on that method first.

What your runes have been placed on does not matter, since the only requirements are that they can be mixed so that they will come up randomly upright or reversed, face up or face down. If you have runes on stones and put those in a bag, you need only shake the bag and reach in the bag and grab a rune quickly for as many times as you need runes. Sticks can be shaken in your hand, with some taken out and turned around every once in a while. Cards have to be shuffled so that cards are turned over and upside down with each shuffle.

Starting with the runes in your hands, think of all aspects of your question. Fix the whole thing in your mind as much as possible, and commence to mix the runes. Mix them thoroughly until you have the unmistakable feeling that the question can now be answered.

There may be a bit of time before you get that feeling. If, however, you take too long, it would be best to start again. This may mean going all the way back to devising a question that the runes can answer. Without going into details, different divination systems do better at answering different types of questions because of the way their probability methods and philosophies work. The Tarot can best answer questions about a person's intentions and the results of actions than the actions themselves, e.g. it is useless to ask what a person is going to do using the Tarot. The *I Ching* is best equipped to answer questions about a person's actions and the results of their actions but not their motivations for what they've done. The runes slot in in that they are best designed for questions about a person's intentions and their actions rather than the results of actions. In Germanic paganism, just like Zoroastrianism, the end of things was fixed and human response was limited to what they intended and did.

When you have difficulty with getting an answer from the runes, there can be many reasons, like any means of divination. Your own tiredness is probably the main reason. However, it may indicate other problems. It is always a good idea to periodically check your divination with a question like, 'Can and will you now provide true and faithful answers to my queries?' Take one rune. If this is positive, go ahead. If the rune is negative, put the runes away and come back to them later.

Let's assume everything is going well, and the runes will now answer your question. They can now be laid out like a Tarot spread. You can use any one of the many spreads suggested in the various books on the Tarot, or you can make up your own. Indeed, you can avoid giving fixed meanings to your spread at all and simply pull out a series of runes. In this the number of runes might be fixed, as in Tacitus' description, or you can continue to choose runes until you feel the question is answered. These more intuitive methods, though, should be used only when you are well familiar with divination by the runes.

Let's take an example of a spread. The question is, 'Will [name of a couple] have improved financial circumstances in the current financial year?' Since we're only talking about a family budget, we'll ascribe the question to the first category, second form. The significator is feoh, the brown rune in Freyja's aettir.

When the runes are drawn, we'll give them the following meanings shows in figure 5.1 below.

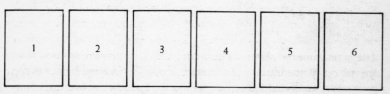

Figure 5.1

Meanings:

1. What they can do to help themselves.
2. What constraints they work with.
3. What is working in their favour.
4. What is working against them.
5. Whether they really desire the improvements mooted in the question.

In this way we angle the meaning of the divination to their intentions (worthiness) and actions more than simply the results. We have concentrated as much on what they are inclined to do as what any particular action might result in. To parallel with the Tarot, if you were to ask 'if I do this, will such-and-such happen?' the Tarot does not consider if you will actually do this. The runes will.

When I did the divination, the answer I got was as follows in figure 5.2.

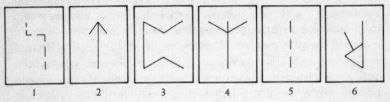

Figure 5.2

So the runes were:

1. Ger face down
2. Tyr face up upright
3. Poerdh face up upright
4. Eolh face up upright
5. Isa face down
6. Rad face up reversed

The significator has not come up among the runes chosen, so conditions are still fairly flexible and can change. This is reinforced by ger in the first position. It indicates this is a time for sowing for improved conditions rather than reaping them. Though their hands are tied at the moment, something they will do in the 1985-86 financial year will result in eventual returns of some usefulness.

Tyr in the second position indicates the current restraints are just and correct. There will be no chance of forcing their way out of current conditions, but negotiation may be of some advantage. Negotiation might mean a rise in wages or an application for a second job.

When looking at poerdh in the third position, we find some reason for concern. It indicates a time of crisis, of judgement. Again, the fluidity of the present situation is suggested, since this rune shows a number of options being open to them, each of which will affect things for a long time to come. Given the rune ger in the first position, it enforces the belief that there are certain opportunities for this couple's financial problems to be eased or eliminated all together.

What stands against these efforts is shown in having eolh face up upright in the fourth position. Since this is a positive rune it may seem a bit strange to find it in this position. But remember that the runes don't have the same philosophy as the Tarot, and answer questions from a different perspective. What this rune shows is a position of happiness, that is, the couple is happy enough. They may be financially strapped, but in a situation that never produces enough of a crisis to truly motivate them we can expect few changes.

This same concept flows into isa in the fifth position. This shows that they are concentrating of friendship, not money. It is enjoyment now that is the focus of their lives. Compare this with tyr in the second position, and we find their constraints exist because they aren't willing to make the sort of effort that would solve their problems.

In the sixth position is rad showing what could overcome that inertia. Again, it is not a crisis of money but of faith. It is a sudden need to stop and say, 'what am I doing?'. It indicates that only this change in attitude can change the financial problem, and only this sort of crisis will trigger that sort of change. Only the change in attitude will mean they deserve greater wealth. Again, with tyr in the second position, we discover that their constraints are largely self-imposed. It is not lack of income, but their spending patterns that is the major source of the problem.

In other words we've got a cycle where the money gets tight but is not an emergency. The urge is to get more, but any new money is quickly spend on non-strategic items. This puts them in exactly the same position they were in the first place. The only way out of this is a true crisis in faith. This crisis must be something that takes away the concentration on others/friendship/good times/etc. which provides the trigger to this overspending cycle.

Once the crisis comes, it will eliminate the problem-that-causes-the-problem. The steps they take to solve that crisis will have far-reaching effects in their lives, as shown by poerdh in the third position. This indicates when this cycle is broken the problem will be solved permanently. We could go further and ask about the crisis or the problem-behind-the-problem, but we've shown the viewpoint of the runes, and can leave it at that for now.

For the moment, let's look at a question answered when the runes chosen don't have a set meaning. In this case, we'll use the question, 'what efforts does a person have to make to become proficient in casting the runes?' This question belongs to the third category of the first form, giving us tyr as the significator. In this case the runes were chosen in the same order and number as opposite in figure 5.3. Note that in this case the significator has appeared among the runes chosen.

1. Eohl face up reversed
2. Manu face up upright
3. Poerdh face down reversed
4. Ehwis face up upright
5. Ing face down reversed
6. Feoh face down upright
7. Tyr face down upright
8. Gyfu face down
9. Lagu face down reversed

The top line shows a person who wants to learn. It's a description of someone just starting out and shows their strengths and weaknesses. The heart of this line (manu) shows the position of the beginner as being between needs of patience with others and a charitable reminder

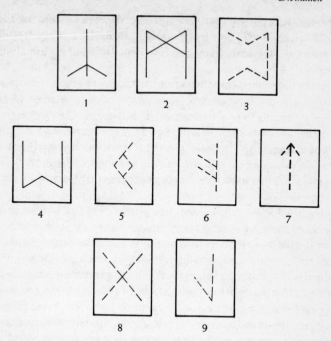

Figure 5.3

that a diviner is also to be an uplifter versus the problem of collapse on the other. Divination by the runes is one system that collapses in on itself. The prediction changes events which changes what should be predicted, and so on *ad infinitum*. Moreover, you cannot allow yourself to be so patient with someone that they fall into a state of decay, since this is one of the ends a divination collapsing on itself can result in. You must bring out the final, best result.

In the second line we see what is possible and not possible. In beginning any runic divination there is a need for tenacity, courage, and determination. This is because, like Jung's approach to examine the meaning of a person's dream, you have never seen a divination quite like the one you're about to do (ehwis). You also need the basic talent for rune divination and not everyone does, and of those who do have it, you must not attempt to use the runes for illicit gain or criminal intent. To do this is to invite retribution from higher powers.

You should realize that the runes have a power separate from you (feoh). They must be coaxed, not commanded. You must live up to their standards to gain their fruits. This is part of the dictum that a gift demands a gift; for the gift of an answer you must give the gift of right action. This shows where the fears of ing reversed show up again with the mention of the danger of moral collapse (tyr). The message reinforces itself that the runes accept you only within certain constraints.

In the final line we have warnings of the things to watch out for. The first of these is physical fatigue (gyfu). Never try prediction when physically tired or emotionally distraught. For some women (and only some) this would mean avoiding divination when mensing.

There is also worry about projecting the past onto the future (lagu). Do not assume that what seems logical from past events will necessarily be correct. The whole point of divination is to be able to supplement or even countermand past-based logic. Again, this means it is necessary to take each divination on its own terms. Just because in a previous divination certain runes meant such-and-such doesn't mean the same interpretation will hold again. We should base our lessons on the past, we should never base our future on the past. This is as true in life as in the runes.

Note that this reading largely consists of a concrete list of what not to do and a few principles or virtues that must be applied. This is very much in keeping with the divinatory emphasis of the runes. Pagan law came up from the people via an assembly called the *thing*. Laws were boundaries, not directives. The methods of rune reading similarly have laws or boundaries and some expected virtues.

At the end of this chapter I'll provide a few more examples of spreads, but any number can be culled from Tarot books. You should remember that each spread may also be adapted for casting of lots. One spread particularly well suited to this is the one shown opposite in figure 5.4.

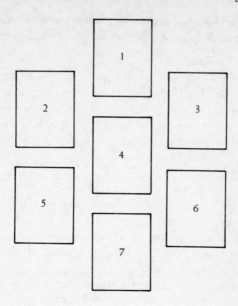

Figure 5.4.

1. Muspell—That which is right, what purification you need, what the powers of the fates require of you.

2. Vanaheim—Things working in your favour, the factors of expansion, growth, fertility, and pleasure.

3. Asgard—Factors of force and strength. If badly aspected it shows weakness. Warnings of what has not been taken into account but should have been. Conflict and strife.

4. Midgard—The core of the question, the querent.

5. Swartalfheim—Skill, purpose, and ability. Hopes and dreams. Indicates the drives that impel the person to ask the question or seek the goal the question implies.

6. Jotunheim—Dangers and forces opposing the querent. Check carefully how the rune in this position relates to the rune in Asgard. In this position are the effects of greed, anger, fear, etc.

7. Niflheim—Things which are not as they seem, the hidden factor.

Fears and hidden forces at work. The querent's weaknesses. Often this is the gift demanded of the querent.

We'll take an example. Take the question, 'Will N. be happy in her chosen profession?' In this we're looking at happiness, so the significator is in Freyja's aettir. The question is in the third form, so the rune will be yellow. The signficator is thus ken. In this case, we'll introduce a small ritual that can help you in your divination. It is very useful for 'macro' questions—those which take in a great many people or world events or simply a great many years. It can, however, also be used from 'micro' questions.

Start by facing north, whether you are sitting, kneeling, or standing matters little so long as you are facing as exactly north as possible. Close your eyes and visualize a great ash tree looming before you. The tree is thousands of miles high and it points its trunk straight through the northern pole star. This is the great ash, Yggdrasil, and its boughs reach over the stars.

You are standing by one root of that great tree, and that root is taller than a skyscraper. And in one of the crooks of that root is a well over twenty feet across. The waters of the well are deep and clear and, if you could touch and taste them, would be cold and fresh.

Next to the well, the Well of Urd, are the three Norns. They are ancient women in dyed wool cloth, and they dictate the fates of men and gods alike. Their names are Urd (Fate), Skuld (Being), and Verthandi (Necessity). They are flanked on either side by the gods and goddesses of Asgard and Vanaheim. As you look through the ranks you will see Odin, Thor, Freyja, Freyer, Frigga, Tyr, Nerthus, and others. When you have established this vision clearly in your mind, turn to the gods and recite the following:

Aesir and Vanir of unbounded realms,
I have come o'er the bifrost to speak with the Norns.

Now turn to the Norns, themselves.

Urd, Verthandi, and Skuld,
Under Yggdrasil's boughs I speak,

that thou wilt answer my questions.
Let me drink from thy well,
that my queries shall be heard.
By the hammer, by the spear,
and by the sacred wagon.

When the Norns nod, open your eyes and mix the runes. You then wait until you have a feeling that they are mixed in a way that will answer your question. Stop mixing and spread or cast them, as the case may be. In the question we've given, 'Will N. be happy in her chosen profession?' we got the following answer.

1. Muspel—ur face down reversed.
2. Vanaheim—doerg face down
3. Asgard—ken face down reversed
4. Midgard—eohl face up upright
5. Swartalfheim—sighel face down
6. Jotunheim—poerdh face down reversed
7. Niflheim—manu face down reversed

The short answer to the query would seem to be, no, she will not be happy. But, equally, there is an element of herself that she can separate from her work and that part of herself she can keep happy. However, note that all runes but one were face down. This would tend to indicate a number of hidden forces at work, which would in turn strengthen the indication that there is something separate from work which applies here. Note that both ken (the significator) and manu are in the spread. We are thus dealing with strong and fairly inflexible forces in this divination.

Ur face down in the first position shows impotence and an inability to move. It is a key of frustration, a period of pause. In other words, before any promotion or job development can occur, there will be a time of treading water. Since this person works in a Government department where promotions are few, this would seem entirely logical. It seems there will be no happiness from development or promotion in the near future.

However, doerg face down in the Vanaheim position shows that there are new developments forthcoming. Just as ur in its position shows a time for sowing, not reaping, so doerg here indicates a period of training and development. This is working in her favour quite clearly since doerg is a positive rune *and* all three yellow runes are in this divination. Perhaps there will be a sudden change in her career, or even a change in careers.

We should also take note of a destructive streak working against this person, though. In finding happiness, this person is their own worst enemy. We again have the suggestion (as with ur) to pull back and think things through. Here we have a person who is not playing the game of the bureaucrat.

In Midgard we have the only rune which is face up, and that's eohl upright. This represents the core of the matter, the querent, and shows this person to be happy in their own right and who can climb to the top. It shows (eventual) attainment and happiness, a person who is ultimately happy in their career.

The rune sighel in Swartalfheim shows the drives that impels this person, and there seem to be many of them. Again we have the suggestion that this person pulls back to think things through. This person is headlong in life, but lacks any plans. This lack of coherence means this person tries to juggle too many acts, and therefore fails to apply herself towards career goals. If a few activities were dropped, things would be much easier.

In Jotunheim we have what is perhaps the harshest of the runes, poerdh face down reversed. It is an indicator that before eventual success will come the natural results of an untenable position. There will be defeat, chaos, and collapse. In other words, the runes are predicting (as the *I Ching* or Tarot would not) that this person's present course of actions will lead to disaster, but that this person will veer from those actions. The runes have even gone so far as to outline how that variation will come about and in what direction things will go.

This warning of collapse is also described by manu face down reversed in Niflheim. This shows a lust for power, a greed in the position of fears and hidden forces. So though this person is driven, it is a drive to achieve too much at once. This person expects too much of herself.

This drive will naturally lead to disaster, since it leads this person to attempt too much. When that collapse comes, this person will reassess, take new stock of the situation. Indeed, it is probable the collapse will be exactly that, a collapse. It is unlikely the collapse will come in work itself. This is because this individual, in blocking off part of their life from work, will not have direct problems in work. The job will go fine, if not offer any satisfaction or promotion. The collapse will be in this person's personal life, and may come as physical exhaustion or similar ailment.

This person would be well advised to think things through now. However, the runes indicate this is very unlikely.

Once you've practised spreading the runes, attention will turn quite naturally to casting them. Proceed to casting only when the spreads are mastered. Though there seems to be little difference, interpreting the runes when cast is far harder than when they are laid on a spread one by one.

Just as there are a number of spreads, so there are a number of layouts for casting. Indeed, any design for spreads can be adapted for casts. The parallels aren't exact, however. For example, one of the simplest and probably hardest layouts for casting the runes is shown below in figure 5.5.

Figure 5.5

Simply stand in the circle and toss the runes into the air. The whole thing can be marked out by string or chalk in a couple of seconds. Simply look at the runes when they land. The closer they are to you, the more significant they are in the divination. Any runes that land on or over the line are excluded from the divination.

It is in fact the simplicity that makes the layout so hard to use. No position has any particular meaning. Each rune must be carefully interpreted not simply in relation to where it falls but where it falls in relation to yourself and the other runes. The whole process can be quite complex and is not suitable for an introductory work like this.

Instead, we'll use the spread already given and use it for casting runes. This will point out the basic differences between spreading the runes and casting them as a lot. As before, we'll perform the small rite described above. The pattern we need can be marked on the floor with chalk, string, or pieces of paper. The size matters little, so long as you remember the wider you cast the runes the larger your layout must be. The question this time is, 'Will H.R. enjoy good health in 1987?' The significator is os. When we cast the runes we get the result shown in figure 5.6.

1. In Muspell we have os face down reversed.
2. In Vanaheim we have thorn face down reversed.
3. In Asgard we have no runes at all.
4. In Midgard we have doerg face up and ken face up reversed.
5. In Swartalfheim we have no runes at all.
6. In Jotunheim we have odel face up reversed.
7. In Niflheim we have ur face up upright, eohl face down reversed, and tyr face up reversed.

The significator, os, is in Muspell, so we are dealing with strong forces in this casting. Os shows there is real reason to be concerned about health in 1987. Troubles with health are likely to be self-imposed and have a fair bit to do with the mental state. This is a period of depression and a sense of loss. Yet, this depression marks the breakdown of barriers that should be broken down. The depression will be temporary, and quite possibly a natural part of readjustment.

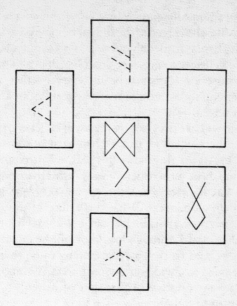

Figure 5.6

With thorn in Vanaheim we have an indication of some sort of pollution. This might be an element of the depression just mentioned, or it might be an improper diet. A visit to the doctor would ensure correct diet. A course of vitamins and some exercise to sweat out the problem would seem advisable.

From the lack of runes in Asgard it would seem this person has very little resistance to what is happening. But equally, a lack of weak runes in this position indicates there are no major health problems in this year. We are looking at things like running colds, the development of an allergy, or some such difficulty. This is supported from the runes in Midgard.

In Midgard, which is the core of the matter, we have doerg face up and ken face up reversed. We thus have an indication of a culmination of matters and complete success (doerg) coupled with an indication of shyness and an unwillingness to use one's own abilities. When we look back at Muspell we realize the difficulties in health seem largely self-imposed. There is some inhibition this person has in using their body's natural defences to preserve good health at all times. Perhaps this person isn't seeking personal health—perhaps they are working towards something so powerfully that physical health actually takes something of a back seat.

In Jotunheim we have odel face up reversed, indicating the existence of help from others which we can see had been lacking to date. The lack of runes in Asgard also shows this person is strongly influenced by those around them. Where before we thought there might be some pollution, we can now see that if there is any problem, it is likely to hinge on this very openness. What the nature of this openness is, however, depends on the person. It could indicate anything from going with the 'wrong' crowd, through loss (as might be indicated from os reversed), or it could be that part of training to be an adept which can leave one open to a wide variety of sources. We may have a hint of entering into the prestage of that state of being.

When we turn to Jotunheim, we see three runes, and these show inspiration (ur), opening to outside forces (eohl), and the need to fight for one's own honour (tyr). All this is in the position of hidden forces, the gift demanded of this person. It indicates that there will be an opening to outside forces, but that this is not the whole of the matters of health.

What will result is a running series of minor ailments, with one major complaint such as a sprain, broken bone, or food poisoning. However, there is an element of the voluntary to this, and knowledge of what is happening could easily shift the balance. The voluntary aspect is shown by the runes in Midgard and the significator in Muspell. Therefore it is likely that the ailments will not interrupt anything of any true importance to this individual, they will exist only enough to be annoying at the time, or to slow this person down while they live through a readjustment in their life.

The above should give you a general idea of how divination by the runes is perfomed. The principles are fairly simple, but take some practice to master. You will have to learn how to ask several questions to get different elements of a situation and put together the answers in a single scenario. You will also, if you are truly serious about divination, learn the runes as part of a range of divinatory practices. The method of divination you use should always be tailored to the question you want answered. Just like the *I Ching*, the Tarot, geomancy, the pendulum, astrology, numerology, or trance writing, the runes are an invaluable source of information about the future.

To round off this chapter, we'll look at a few spreads suitable for use with the runes.

Spreads and Casts

To begin, we'll use a spread already familiar to users of the Tarot. It's the Celtic spread invented by A.E. Waite, a member of the Golden Dawn magical fraternity. The runes should be laid out as shown in figure 5.7 overleaf. If you have stones that won't allow one to ride over the other, place rune two below rune one, but at a ninety degree angle so it can be distinguished.

1. The querent and their situation. The situation as it is.
2. What opposes the querent. The source of opposition can be internal or external.
3. The foundation the querent is working from. It is often events in the distant past, but can also be training, skills, or talent.
4. Recent events which are still influencing the querent's thoughts, feelings, and intentions.
5. The best path the querent can take.
6. The path the querent is now most likely to take. It can often be taken as the path the querent would have taken had there been no divination by the runes.
7. This is the querent as an individual. This is their talents, drives, and predilections.
8. This is the situation itself. This is what would happen if the querent were not involved.

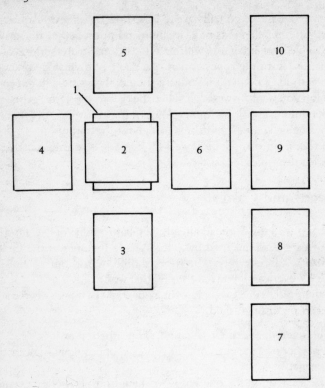

Figure 5.7

9. The querent's hopes and fears.
10. The final outcome the querent is most likely to achieve given all the influences above. This is not a final event, but the course of greatest probability.

The aettir spread is equally useful as a spread and for casting. The spread follows in figure 5.8.

1. Freyja's aettir—Matters of love, happiness, and creativity and how these affect the querent. What the querent wants.

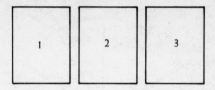

Figure 5.8

2. Heimdall's aettir—The querent's avenues for achievement, the opportunites for success, wealth, and victory. It also deals with whether the person deserves to get what they want, and whether what they want is what they need.

3. Tiwaz's aettir—The spiritual and intellectual aspects of the question. It describes what binds Fate has cast around the matter.

When casting as lots, the same meanings can be used in either a triangle or a circle. These are shown below in figure 5.9.

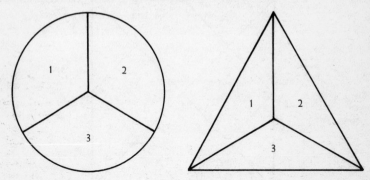

Figure 5.9

Finally, the zodiac can be used as a spread or for casting, and can be inscribed in either the circular or the mediaeval (square) version. These are shown in figures 5.10 and 5.11, respectively.

1. Aries—first house—This is the querent himself; their personal appearance, their personality, their health, and their position in the question asked.

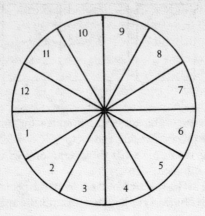

Figure 5.10

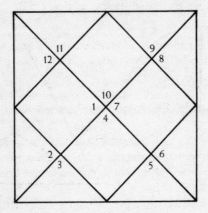

Figure 5.11

2. Taurus—second house—Monetary and financial matters, how dependent on money the querent will be in the area of the question, the wealth and success of any projects, generally.

3. Gemini—third house—Deals with the areas of communications, short trips, studies, speeches and eloquence, publicity and agencies.

It provides details of how important they will be and how successful the querent will be in using them.

4. Cancer—fourth house—The effects of the house, family (especially the mother), home environment and, where necessary, retirement of the querent.

5. Leo—fifth house—Describes the querent's hopes and fears, chances of success, and the amorous areas of life. It covers love affairs, childbirth, courtship, and recreation and how they impinge on the querent's hopes and chances of success.

A note of warning; if thorn or poerdh are in this house, abandon the divination, it is worthless.

6. Virgo—sixth house—The effects of hierarchy and health, and in particular how subordinates (including bureacrats) will help or hinder the querent reach their goal. It also shows whether sickness should be taken into account.

7. Libra—seventh house—How deals, partners, or the spouse will affect the situation.

8. Scorpio—eighth house—Covers death, inheritance, and similar aspects. Includes the areas of natural talents, inherited property or legacies, and social position in relation to the querent.

9. Sagittarius—ninth house—Dreams, visions, and inspiration and how they affect the question at hand. Can also relate to migration or long-term journeys.

10. Capricorn—tenth house—Reputation, profession and career, and life's work are all described in this position. Shows how they will aid or hinder the querent's hopes and fears, or make the querent forget particular directions altogether.

11. Aquarius—eleventh house—Shows things that work for the querent, but also covers social position, philanthropy, idealism, and what role the querent is seeing for himself. Often a good house to look at to see why the querent is going for a particular goal if the goal being asked about is a stepping stone to the querent. If the querent thinks money will get a chance to get a woman, this will show the influence of the woman.

12. Pisces—twelfth house—Things that are working against the querent,

particularly secret enemies, but also the idleness or laziness, sloth, anger, greed (etc.) of the querent, himself. This house will show if the querent will get what they want and then regret that success ever afterward.

Note of warning; again, thorn or poerdh in this house means the divination is useless. Abandon the question for at least a day and better for a week.

These are a few forms of the many spreads and casts available for use with the runes. Other spreads and castings can be gleaned from books on the Tarot, *I Ching*, and similar books of divination. The possibilities are endless, and you should already have a good working knowledge to start you exploring those possibilities. However, to extend your range of vision further, we will examine some of the Germanic godforms, next, a topic not covered in other works on the occult.

CHAPTER SIX

The Godforms of Asgard and Vanaheim

Many books on occultism and magic will tell you about godforms, but they all concentrate exclusively on the deities of Egypt, Pheonicia, Greece-Rome, and a nod to Israel, Babylonia, and Assyria. The Germanic gods have been ignored, despite the wealth they offer to anyone willing to study them. Since this book deals with the powers of those godforms, it is essential that we learn rather more about them, particularly since the Germanic godforms are different from the godforms of the above traditions.

The basic method of assuming a godform is simple enough. You begin by learning all you can about a particular god. This means reading the myths in which that deity is invoked and learn to understand them esoterically. This means examining the myths to know the various associations and attributes that apply to that deity; learn the ritual content that lays behind a number of myths. Where there are rituals evident, participate in those rituals. Build the image in your mind as strongly as possible. When you've done this, begin to imagine the myths in your mind in every detail, imagine them as if they were happening here and now. When you have built up so strong an understanding of the deity whose godform you wish to assume that you enter into the myths as you imagine them, the time has come to assume the godform, itself.

For this you will need to sit in a comfortable chair that will allow you to keep your feet flat on the floor, and to rest the palms of your hands either on your thighs or on armrests such that your forearms are parallel with the ground. Begin breathing rhythmically; breathe in to a count of four, hold your breath for a count of four, exhale for a count of four, hold your lungs empty for a count of four, and repeat. Always hold your breath by your diaphram, not by closing your nasal passages. The actual numbers of the breathing do not matter, so long as each stroke is even, that is, you should hold your breath for as long as you breathe in or out. You will maintain this regimen of breathing throughout the rest of the exercise.

When the breathing is established, recite the following invocation.

I call upon the powers of N----,
I call upon the strength, the wisdom, the power.
I take thy name, oh, N----,
Grant me to descend from thine abode,
and fill me with thy energies,
for I am worthy of thy power.

Next begin playing in your mind the various attributes you know about the god. Think of the god's functions in the pantheon, the associations built up. Dress yourself with the significant attributes of the deity. If you're adopting the godform of Thor, place the gloves on your hands, hold the hammer itself. Wear the belt and feel it double your strength. When this process is done, begin imagining yourself with the powers and knowledge of that god. Visualize yourself *as* that god in each of the myths you've learned. When this is done you should see the image of the god surrounding you, normally as a form slightly larger than yourself but occupying the same space. You should feel a surge of energy and strength with this final adopting of the form.

Then, in the name of that god, exercise the powers you need. When this is done and you wish to reverse the process, use the following dismissal.

I now lay aside the powers of the god N----,
and resume my role as [your name],
who is happy, healthy, and wise,
and in every way worthy of the gods' favour,
for every part of me is divine,
if I but attain to the balance.

Then lay down each attribute of the god with thanks. Let the powers return to the higher realms from whence they came. Let the image around you fade as it returns to its realm. Finally, break the rhythmic breath by breathing in deeply, holding it for an instant, and breathing out with the thought that you are closing the exercise. Then recite.

So be it.

If you are keeping a diary, put any notes into it now. Otherwise, go immediately to do something completely different. You should always 'clear your head' after practising a form of magic. That being said, we can now turn our attentions to the various godforms themselves. In this book I've limited discussion to a few of the major forms rather than discuss all forms.

The one thing that should be noted about Germanic godforms is they cover a wider area of topics and interests than the Greco-Roman, Israeli, or Egyptian godforms. The Germanic tribes accepted gods as being a person's cult for a lifetime, so the godforms tended to extend wider than those of other pantheons where individual gods served individual functions in a person's life, and the person was expected to provide devotion to several deities in a lifetime.

Because of this, various deities have different forms to them. We've already seen in chapter two how Odin has different layers to him. His godforms are, in fact, shaman, psychopompous, and Allfather. Similarly, Loki has four forms; trickster, bound giant, chief of evil, and companion. These sorts of forms are more than different duties, as was the case in Thoth's custodianship of wisdom and inventor of writing. They are different aspects of power each relating to the different archetypal powers the gods was associated with. In this discussion, I have limited myself to the more useful godforms available, though the picture would have been incomplete if I hadn't made some mention of those godforms (e.g. Hel) whom you must know in order to protect yourself from them, but which you should not use, yourself.

Odin

Animals: Wolf, raven   *Rune*: Os
Tree: Ash   *Weapon/tool*: the spear
Symbol: the valknut

Odin has already been extensively discussed in chapter two, so there is little extra to go into here. The godform we will look at first is the shaman. In this form he can be invoked for anything to do with inspiration, poetry, communication with the dead, and prophesy. He is cunning and able to bind or loose people from all sorts of fetters, physical and mental. He is also the god of wisdom.

When using this godform, imagine him as a tall man (at least six feet four inches or taller) who has hair in a tangled grey mane down to his shoulders. He wears leather breeches or trousers which are tied at the sides of the legs rather than sewn. He is usually bare-chested, with a cloak of animal skin and a broad-rimmed black hat which is pulled down over the right eye. He carries a blackthorn staff which is sometimes shown as in flower with small white buds on it. The staff is carved with eighteen runes.

As the Allfather, Odin is the lord of hosts and the giver of victory. He is the god of the nobles, and hence is the god to call on in respect of titles, position, wealth, inheritance, and property. He is, however, something of a treacherous god, and many myths show him giving victory to those who do not deserve it. He is not to be trusted when dealing with questions of combat unless he is given his share of the spoils. Even then there should be doubt in your mind. Odin the Allfather is also an all-seeing god, and hence can be called upon for divination and inspiration of a rather more concrete form than the god of inspiration.

In this form he wears a fine mailcoat of black leather with brass metal rings. His helmet has two horns on top of it, and a metal eye-patch of the right side. He carries the spear Gungnir, which is slightly taller than he is, and has a three-bladed point which is designed to look a bit like a raven. He has a raven on each shoulder and two wolves by his feet. His hair is still steel-grey and lies about his shoulders. He wears animal-skin trousers and boots, with metal rings around the boots.

To summon him, he has the symbol of the *valknut*, or knot of the slain, and the triceps. These are shown below, respectively, in figure 6.1.

Figure 6.1.

Thor

Animals: Goat, bear   *Rune*: Rad
Tree: Oak   *Weapon/tool*: the hammer
Symbol: the hammer, swastika, and sunwheel

Where Odin was a god of the nobility, Thor was a god of the middle class; the independent or yeoman farmer, the trader, and the adventurer often gave him allegience. His essential purpose for ritual work is hallowing though most of the myths involving him show him defending Midgard and Asgard from giants and monsters. Today he is remembered mostly as a god of thunder.

He is invoked for hallowing, community, to aid trade and sea travel (particularly migration or long journeys), and to raise or quell storms. He is a god of the oath. Because of his connection with rain, he is invoked for the fertility of crops, and from that an increase in business generally—a deity of the small businessman, in modern terms. He can also be invoked when seeking a place to live or fairness in a business deal.

He should be pictured above all else as big. He is nearly as big as a giant, and is best seen as seven or eight feet tall. He has flaming red hair and blue eyes which are quite piercing. He often goes bare-headed but is sometimes seen as wearing an iron helmet. He wears a heavy cloth shirt which sometimes gives way to a bearshirt. His legs are bare and he wears animal-skin boots. On his hands are gloves of gold with which he controls his hammer, *mjollnir*. This hammer is like a small sledgehammer with a very short handle, with a ring in the end of that handle. This is made of gold, like the gloves. Thor wears a belt, also of gold, which doubles his strength. On one arm he wears a ring of silver, people can take oaths on this ring.

Thor is associated with a number of symbols and devices which often reflect the multiplicity of roles and forms he has. I have ignored Thor the chariot god, the god of thunder and storms. This form is of Thor the hallower. The hammer was often called upon to hallow births, initiations, marriages, feasting and death. And although some cremation was used, Thor's followers were normally buried at death. Some thought they would live in a specific place underground, such as a particular mountain—a natural enough ritual development, since Thor's mother was the Earth.

The sign of the hammer is significant to Thor. His followers made the sign of the hammer in the air and wore its likeness in silver around their necks. The sign was used in prayer and in blessing meals much as Christians still use the cross today.

As a god of lightning, the hallowing element of fire also became important in his cult. A torch carried around some land hallows it, and at some of Thor's temples there was a sacred fire which was never allowed to go out. But this was part-and-parcel with the thunder god.

The signs of Thor are the hammer, the deosil swastika, and the sunwheel, which are shown in this order in figure 6.2.

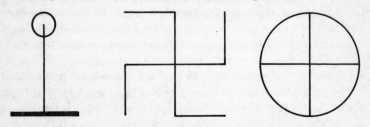

Figure 6.2

In figure 6.3 we have the directions to use when inscribing Thor's hammer into the air. This is always done over food or your drink before consuming it. You inscribe the ring first, then the handle, and finally the head, as follows.

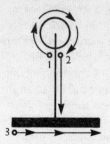

Figure 6.3

Freyer

Animals: Horse, boar   *Rune*: Ing
Tree: Yew   *Weapon/tool*: Plough
Symbol: the ship

Freyer is one of twins, his sister being Freyja. Divine twins went back far in Germanic paganism, and helps show how ancient this deity is. This is also shown by the fact that although Freyer's protection is sought in battle, he is not a war god. He is a god of peace, plenty, joy, and devotion. He is a fertility god and a god of resurrection.

Freyer can be invoked for the sun, rain, and harvest. He can make fields fertile and the crops strong. He provides families with children, and sanctions marriages within the community. He is the patron of festivals and common activities, charity, and communal activities that are apolitical.

As a godform, Freyer should be visualized as a man just past youth—in his forties—who is slightly under six foot in height or slightly taller than the person summoning him, whichever is greater. He is red-haired and bearded, and is lithe and fit. He wears a white, woollen sleeveless jerkin and breeches and boots. He has a metal ring of silver on his arm like Thor. He has very little body hair. Around his waist is a black leather belt and a jewelled scabbard which is empty.

Among the pagan Germans, Freyer was worshipped by mystery plays which seem to have included a theme of death and resurrection. There was also dancing and ringing of bells among his worshippers, and this led to other pagans not in his cult looking down upon his followers everywhere but Sweden. In Sweden Freyer was becoming the chief deity by the close of the pagan period. Perhaps his followers were the ecologists and pacifists of their day. His worship also included games and feasts, which were a common worship at the time. However, it is notable that a priestess would take an image of the god around in a cart or wagon to attend these festivals.

His symbols are the ship, the cart, and the phallus, all symbols dealing with both fertility and the transmigration of the soul. A common belief about Freyer, and another godform, was of a miraculous child who came along in a ship to the shore of a new land, carrying a sheaf of grain in his hand. The child would be the source of rejoicing, become the king of the land and bring peace and prosperity with his reign. Sometimes he returns by sea, other times he is killed and dismembered. If killed, he is mourned over, and parts of his body may be sent to different parts of the kingdom. But he does not become resurrected; the formula is lunar, not solar. He was succeeded by his son, and the cycle continued.

Freyja

Animals: Boar, falcon, calf, chicken   *Rune*: Feoh
Tree: Pine or evergreen   *Weapon/tool*: none
Symbol: Necklace of amber

Above all else, Freyja is a goddess of love and is invoked for seduction, courting, and marriage. She blesses children and gives girls in marriage. She ensures safe and healthy childbirth. She is a goddess of plenty and fruitfulness, and can be invoked by those wanting healing or good health. She can also bestow wealth. She is a patron of astral projection and divination, her knowledge of the latter apparently coming from the dead, but this aspect of her it is best to avoid.

In the necromantic form she has a greed for wealth and can kill by magic. She is an entrapping goddess—better to stay with her side of lust and love, though here there is a wild and exuberant side of her.

In her light side, she shares many functions with her brother Freyer. Anything to do with marriage and fertility that one of these two deal with, the other one can deal with as well.

Freyja should be visualized as a woman in her early to mid-twenties who wears boots of brown calfskin, gloves of white calfskin, and a hood of catskin that covers her hair. She wears linens of white embroidered pleasantly with gold thread. This dress does not cover her legs. She has a cloak that reaches to the ground that is made of hawk's feathers. Her face is beautiful to look at, with flashing eyes and full red lips. She should be visualized as being in a cart which is drawn by large black cats with green eyes. The cats are an intimation of the disturbing side to her nature, since this is less divided from her other godforms than other deities are separated from their darker godforms.

Freyja was celebrated at feasts at which there was dancing and singing. A chorus would be used to put one or more priestesses into an ecstatic trance. These priestesses, these volvas, would then answer questions from the crowd; these questions were about the future, such as coming crops, marriages, and so on. Freyja's worship may have also involved and ritual marriage which, as part of the rite, was consumated. It seems certain Freyja was known to have been wild and reckless many times, and is known to have gained her magic necklace by sleeping each night in turn with the four dwarves who made it.

In imitation of her, her followers wore necklaces in imitation of Freyja's own amber-beaded *Brisingamen*. This necklace is connected with life and the dead, and it should be noted that half the dead slain in battle went to Freyja, while the other half went to Odin.

Freyja's symbols are the boar and the vulva. The boar symbol should be seen from the side and should be two-dimensional, as seen below in figure 6.4.

Figure 6.4

Frigga

Animals: Falcon　　　　　　*Rune*: Boerc
Tree: Apple, birch　　　　　*Weapon/tool*: Net
Symbol: the cup

Frigga or Frigg was the wife of Odin, but was also closely associated with Freyja. Where Freyja was the young maiden, Frigga was the wife. She is the fertility goddess, a protector of hearth and home and the patron of fidelity in marriage, and can be invoked for any matter falling under these topics. She can also be called upon for matters of and rites of birth, marriage, and death, and can grant children to childless couples. She is the one who gives children their destiny (which may make her one of the Norns or simply like them), helps girls find mates, and helps women in childbirth. She is a goddess of fertility which transcends life, and her symbols of fruit (especially apples) and nuts ensure a happy after-life. She can also be called upon to ensure an easy death, and she, too, has a dark side.

In another godform, Frigga is the weeping goddess, and gold was often called the tears of Frigga. In this form she is a weaver and is often depicted as working as her loom. She, in this form, is overcast by shadow, but she is also a patron of small business and trades. In this form, too, she is a patron of the solidarity of family life, the strength of the family facing disaster or times of trouble.

When invoked, it is the patron of marriage who should be called. In this form, Frigga should be visualized as a woman with dark hair who is in her thirties to even her early forties. Her hair is bound up and braided with a ring. She wears a green woven cloth and wears many pieces of jewellery in gold and precious stones on her arms, neck, and hands. She is of happy countenance.

Little is positively known of Frigga's worship in pagan times, since the Christians were harder on the goddesses than the gods of the north. However, it does seem clear that her worship was in a sanctuary located on an island. What form this took is hard to discern, though it is likely this physical isle imitated an 'isle of the blessed' where the dead would go to feast in plenty, happiness, and peace forevermore.

In her form as a patron of trade and for strength in adversity, imagine a woman in her late thirties to early forties. She is sitting next to a loom which is half filled with some embroidery or a tapestry. To her other side is an empty cradle. She is weeping tears of gold. But though the gold is molten, it is cool to the touch. She wears a darker green than in her other form, and the jewellery is almost gone. There is only a ring on the hand and a necklace of gold and diamonds. In one hand is often a golden apple.

The symbol of the patroness of marriage is the cup, of strength in adversity is the boar. These are shown in figure 6.5. Note, though, that stylized figures have been presented. It is possible to use the objects, themselves, as symbols.

Figure 6.5

Tiwaz

Animals: Wolf, dog   *Rune*: Tyr
Tree: Ash   *Weapon/tool*: Sword, spear
Symbol: Sword, pillar, or tied cord

Throughout this work I have used 'Tiwaz' and 'Tyr' to distinguish the early pagan sky god from the late pagan war god from the rune of the same name. Tiwaz was one of the earliest of Germanic gods and in many ways a hold-over from the earliest recorded religious notions of the Indo-Iranian people. Indeed, since a basic pattern of religion is the sky god marrying the earth goddess, it may be that Tiwaz fell further in the pagan pantheon than one would normally think.

Tiwaz is, like Odin, a god of warfare, but he is also a god of justice.

He is the god men swear on, and they do this by swearing on their weapons. Should they break their oaths, the god will make those weapons turn on them. Tiwaz can be invoked for all of these. In addition, he is the god of contract and law (much as Mitra was in Zoroastrianism and Hinduism). Thus, Tiwaz is also the god of honesty, good will, justice, and jurisprudence. He in fact is the patron of lawyers and civil servants.

Tiwaz should be visualized as a big man, nearly as tall but not as wide as Thor. He is blond-haired and has blue eyes. His right hand is missing and the stump has not been capped, so the teethmarks of Fenris the wolf can still be seen in the pinkened flesh. His hair is braided and this goes over his left shoulder. He wears a metal helmet with horns on it, sometimes a falcon's wings. He, like Odin, is missing his right eye, but he wears a black leather eye-patch. His other clothes are a jerkin of black or brown leather in which rings are not sewn extravagantly, but just here and there. He carries a sword in his left hand and the sword is marked with the rune tyr. The scabbard is on his right side and both sword and scabbard are plain and unadorned. He wears brown trousers of woven cloth, black boots set with metal rings, and has a cloak of wolfskin, the head of one of the wolves hangs over one shoulder.

Tiwaz's followers wore a cord around their waists, and this is one of the god's three symbols. The symbols help define his godforms.

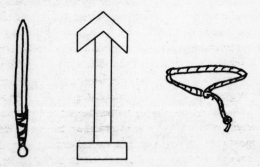

Figure 6.6

The sword is the war god, the pillar the sky god, and the tied cord the god of contracts. All these are bound by the central image of Tiwaz as the god of cosmic justice. These symbols are given in figure 6.6. But, unlike the other deities, the one image can serve to summon any one godform of Tiwaz. This is another indication of his great age. He is quite a suitable godform, since he has the great use of redress of the balances against an overmighty opponent.

Hel

Animals: Monsters and dragons   *Rune*: Thorn
Tree: None   *Weapon/tool*: Knife, cup of blood
Symbol: Gate of Death

As far as we know, Hel went unworshipped in the pagan north, and this was just as well. This is one of those forms you should know about but never use.

Hel is the daughter of Loki and the ruler of Niflheim, the land of the dead. There she received all those who die of old age or disease, and the wicked. Her land is a place of darkness, filled with animated corpses and serpents, notable for a constant stench and a mistiness that prevents anyone from seeing too far. Throughout the halls there is treasure piled high which simply rots—even gold rots in Niflheim.

Hel is only useful for inflicting death, pain, and misery, bringing things to ruin and, occasionally, creating a catharsis that has some therapeutic effect. The same sort of therapy was well known in the Mediaeval Ages—it was called filth therapy. She can also be used to explore the world of the shades.

Hel appears as a totally naked woman. From head to hips she is very beautiful but also very pale. Her skin is almost albino and has no blemishes of any sort. But from the hips down she is a rotting corpse. Her skin is greenish and grey-black and covered with the sores of the rotting. In some places the skin has broken to show a pusy pinkish flesh beneath, and sometimes the break goes as deep as the bone. Insects and maggots crawl all over the lower half of her skin. Since the skin repairs as well as decays, it is always in this sort of state, although the sores migrate across the flesh over time.

Heimdall

Animals: Ram, pig
Tree: Willow and all sea-facing trees
Symbol: Ram's horn

Rune: Hoel
Weapon/tool: Sword

Heimdall and Loki are the most enigmatic characters in the Germanic myths, and many suggestions have been given as to their origin. For example, Heimdall has been suggested to be the personification of Yggdrasil, a son of the ram, the woodpecker god, and so on. But the central image of Heimdall is a god of the cliffs that face the sea and hence the watcher of the gods. It is as watcher that Heimdall is most notable.

As one of the Vanir, Heimdall is a fertility god, but his main uses in invocation are for silencing troubled minds, learning the true nature of things, and gaining wisdom. He can provide plenty, and can also define the orders of things. In this it is significant that Heimdall gives birth to the different classes of Germanic society, according to the myth, the *Song of Rig*.

He should be visualized as a tall man with broad shoulders. He has swarthy skin and hair which is naturally black but which has been bleached by the sun. His hair and beard are both unkempt and his skin is quite leathery. His face, however, is kindly and smiling. He wears a linen shirt and breeches and a sealskin vest or waistcoat. He has a heavy arm-ring on each arm; silver on the right and gold on the left. He has a ram's horn in the right hand and a sword in his left. His shoes are sealskin.

One of the significant aspects of Heimdall is his opposition to Loki, and the two can't entirely be considered separately. One of the clues of their natures, for example, is the fact that they face each other on the final day at ragnarok, while supposedly much more important gods deal with Loki's children. Indeed, Heimdall was said to have fought Loki in the shape of a seal.

Other clues also exist, of course. The very name *Heimdall* shows a connection of land, since heim means land. However, Heimdall was said to be born of nine maidens, which is taken to represent nine waves, and some clues indicate Heimdall was born of the sea itself like Aphrodite. The horn he will sound, *Gjallarhorn*, that will warn the gods of ragnarok's coming is said to be heard in all the nine worlds—the sound that would be heard in all nine worlds would be the sound of the sea crashing against the rocks. Moreover, mountain goats would be found on cliffs near the sea and the use of the ram's horn compounds the symbol. Again, those in myths who give birth to social classes are often sea-deities.

Loki

Animals: None specific   *Rune*: Poerdh
Tree: Maple   *Weapon/tool*: Bow and arrows, darts
Symbol: the grave mound

Loki, like his daughter, is better left unworshipped. He has four basic godforms, and of these only the trickster and the companion do any good. Like Zoroastrianism, Germanic paganism described its evil as being bound underground. In this, Loki is like Ahriman, a bound giant, and this is one of his roles. But he is also a thief who gets the gods into trouble and out again, who gains them their greatest treasures and fathers their greatest enemies, who is known to help destroy them at ragnarok yet is a sworn brother of Odin. All these are part of his character.

He has been thought a trickster figure, a water spirit, a fire spirit, and so on. As we see in his battles with Heimdall, however, the central image of Loki is erosion. He is the god whose struggles to break free fray the shoreline, shift the sands at the beaches, and so on. This is why he and Heimdall fought in the form of seals—seals occupy both land and sea and hence are somewhat a neutral turf on which to fight. Loki as erosion is a thief, taking away good cropland and even the crops themselves.

Note how Loki cuts off Sif's hair, steals the necklace of Freyja, and so on. Loki is a shape-changer just as the dunes by the shore are changed by the sea from day to day. Alluvial action reveals great treasures, often gold, just as Loki gets the gods their greatest treasures which are often of gold.

In this the final destruction is scaled down to day-to-day events so people can handle it. It can even give way to being a figure of fun, and this happens to Loki. Only at the end, when the whole of the land falls into the sea does Loki's true image as a bound giant come out again.

As such, we have gained by occult thought a new insight into these two enigmatic deities.

As for invoking Loki, he is useful only for theft, lies, distortion, and vengeance. He has no social functions, and is only secondarily useful for death, destruction, or pain.

He does, however, have redeeming features in another of his forms, the companion. In this he is useful for travelling, exploration, mining, searching for wealth, and for trade.

In these cases, he is visualized as a handsome man with strange, compelling, and evil eyes. He is clean shaven and has little body hair. His skin is greyish. He wears no shirt, simply leather wristbands and a gold armband on the left arm. He is thin like Odin but not as tall. He wears canvas trousers and goes barefoot. He carries a sword and a dagger in his belt, the sword drips with poison. He has a cloak of animal skins.

Though this form of him is useful, be very careful with it. It demands a gift for a gift quite assiduously. Loki, being greedy, keeps track of what the score is.

Njord

Animals: All sea animals
Tree: None
Symbol: the ship
Rune: Manu
Weapon/tool: Harpoon

Another Vanir, Njord, too, has associations with fertility. Where Aegir is the god personifying the sea, Njord is a deity of the sea and of the fruitfulness of the sea. Thus, though he has a dark side, this is less dangerous and is easier to avoid than Aegir's 'devouring jaws'.

Njord can be invoked for a wide range of purposes which centre on the sea, sea travel, the wealth of the sea, and commerce. He offers safe travel, and hence is patron of commerce and mails and messages.

He controls the winds and the sea and can provide good seafaring, trade, and fishing. He can grant wealth through trade. He can also heal wounds and provide peace and plenty. As in seafaring, so in battle, Njord can provide protection.

Njord is a god of fresh starts, of reincarnation and the transmigration of souls. In this it is significant that his followers, when dead, were buried or, less often, burned in real or model ships. Njord is thus the patron of a happy and fit reincarnation. He is a god for cleansing, of renewal, and of beginning again. The god you turn to to make a fresh start. This includes marriages, since this, too, is a renewal of each partner in the other. He is also a comforter in a time of mourning since that, too, requires a form of cleansing.

He is also an inspiring god, giving his followers good ideas and good advice. And his protection extends to travel, battle, and in quests for knowledge.

Like Freyer and Thor, he can be sworn to by, or on, the silver arm-ring all three shared.

Like all sea gods, he has a devouring side. There are some whom he accepts into his domain. He is as stern as Odin in his command that 'a gift demands a gift'. Thus, though he grants much, he requires fair payment. He is not a god to call upon for an easy route to wealth. Though he is comforting in times of troubles.

Njord should be visualized as a blond-haired, blue-eyed man. His hair is a tangled mane and his beard runs fully down to his waist. He has a laughing expression and kind eyes which yet carry a hint of sadness. His skin is leathery, he has much body hair, and there are many scars

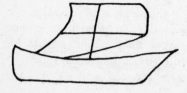

Figure 6.7

on his body. He wears canvas pants, usually of grey, no shirt or shoes. There's silver ring around his right arm, and it's etched with runes. A piece of rope ties his breeches up. On his head is a fillet of leather. He carries a hook in one hand and a net in the other. The net trails after and around him. The hand holding the net is missing a couple of joints.

His symbols are the ship and the arch, which are shown in figure 6.7.

Balder

Animals: Grazing animals, deer   *Rune*: Doerg
Tree: Oak with mistletoe   *Weapon/tool*: Axe
Symbol: Sundisc and axe

There are two literary sources about Balder, and they differ widely in approach and content. The god Balder, though, is from Snorri's account. In this we have a deity of justice and mercy, a deity with clear parallels to both Christ and Mithras. Indeed, Balder does have some parallels to Indo-Iranian thought.

The name 'Balder' comes from a root meaning bright day. Like Tiwaz he is a deity of the sky, but unlike Tiwaz or Tir, he is a god of peace. Thus, he is a god to turn to for justice, for wisdom and mercy. He is also a god of poetry, inspiration, and entertainments, including music. He is a courtly god who can be turned to for matters of love and beauty in all their forms. In particular, he is the god of the love of the adept, the love of all things which is sometimes called agape. He can be invoked for learning, civil law (criminal law belongs to Tiwaz), and obtaining justice.

He should be visualized as a young man not yet in full maturity, and is either clean shaven or lightly bearded. He has bright blue eyes that are as piercing as Thor's or Odin's and bright blond hair. He wears a tunic of yellow linen, with a yellow belt and armbands of gold. He wears a yellow cap on his head and carries a golden battleaxe.

His symbols are the sundisc and the axe, and both are shown in figure 6.8.

By use of godforms, your divination and runic magic can be made

Figure 6.8

more effective. More, they can be used to bring you closer to those powers that the gods represent. They should, however, be used judiciously. Learn the forms one at a time, and master one before you go on to another. Too, learn the magic from your own knowledge, and use the knowledge of magic to improve your understanding of the godforms, themselves. Magical initiation is a cycle, and each aspect becomes a springboard to learning another aspect all the more deeply. Godforms are normally a practice reserved for later development, but the initial understanding of the godforms, as given in this chapter, can be vital to the first steps of practical magic, which is what we look at next.

CHAPTER SEVEN

Talismanic Magic

The Germanic futhark can be the basis for magical practices as diverse, effective, and spiritually fulfilling as any of the traditional approaches of Western magic. Every area of study from divination to talismans, to ritual, to astral projection, can be built from this futhark. However, it is also true that the magic of the futhark is different from that discussed in most books on magic.

It should be realized that the futhark is a method of writing. It has uses apart from magic, and in this differs from the kabbalah or astrology. The futhark is a magic of this world, bound up in the ecology of life and death, where holy and bountiful have not been made separate concepts. Futharkian magic is in this way closer to the magic of Zoroastrianism or Mithrasism.

To the futhark, the world is good and what it offers is good. Though it is tainted with evil, it is never irredeemable. It is only excess, hoarding or cruelty, that the runes will not accept and will react to. So while the runes expect and permit gain, they never allow dominance.

This is because of the principle, 'a gift demands a gift, better not to pledge than to pledge overmuch'. That is, you have to put in proportionately for what you receive. In this we are faced with something like a magical Newtonian law: for every action there is an equal and opposite reaction. In this case, it is that results depend on the magical energy input, and these are proportional. For those with some magical talent, the magical energy is easier than the physical, mental, and emotional work that would otherwise be required. You will in any case still have to gain magical skills by input of exercise, knowledge, and magical power. It is not, in this case, the final balance of things that is at issue, but the efficiency of action and results that makes the difference, and the runes are efficient. They aren't a free ride, but they are an edge.

To begin our studies, then, we will turn to the talismans.

Talismans

The runes are ideally suited to talismans. Their shapes aid the design of aesthetic talismans, and that they are a magical alphabet makes simply writing a magical intent in them a form of magical act in itself. Indeed, this sort of talisman has turned up frequently in archaeology. Runes were used to carve into caskets or mounds particular formulas. They were carved into weapons to give those weapons a magical life of their own. And so on. However, the traditional style of talismans from modern magic is also suitable for runic talismans, and there is no reason to reject it.

Indeed, one basic form of talisman is to simply carve or etch the appropriate rune to your purposes on a weapon, object, or separate talisman. The main thrust of each rune's esoteric meaning, and hence its use in talismans, was given in chapter three. For quick reference, however, I provide the following list of the most useful runes and their uses.

Feoh is useful for money, friendliness, and gaining merit.

Ur is useful when undertaking an adventure or a risky enterprise, such as starting a business.

Os is good for writing poetry, prose, and for public speaking.

Rad is good for travelling in safety, for understanding great changes, and raising and speaking to the dead. It is also good for anything to do with ancestors apart from inheritance.

Ken is good for extending knowledge or when undertaking divination, and to gain knowledge of the secret meaning of things. It's also a good luck charm.

Wynn is good for gaining favour of superiors and for passing tests and exams.

Nyd is good for success generally and to achieve necessary things that seem impossible to achieve.

Isa is good for gaining promotion, election, and for gaining positions of authority generally.

Ger is good for gardening and making plants grow, for farming, for a happy home, and for having good times. On new year's night (whenever you celebrate that), draw ger on the arch over your doorway (front or back, front is preferable) in delible ink (sic). The household will be lucky for as long as the ink remains.

Eolh will provide protection from danger.

Sighel provides knowledge of transcendent powers and clairvoyance. It makes your actions conform with your destiny.

Tyr is useful for gaining courage, strong will, and resolution. This was the rune carved on people's weapons, and it is still useful when seeking aid in a fight; physical, legal, or moral.

Boerc is good for healing and keeping good health, it aids in the atonement for misdeeds, and calms troubled minds.

Ehwis is good for calling upon divine aid and for finding help from unusual or unlooked-for sources. It is another good luck charm.

Manu helps in the essential quest of the existentialist; to understand thyself.

Lagu is good for community and binding people to oneself. It also helps in finding and retaining lovers. However, those who use the rune for retaining lovers will soon find it is they who start changing, not the lover who is dominated. The runes force this change to avoid disbalance, and hence avoid, too, a practice of fixation, which is common to many acts of black magic.

Ing is useful for gaining the respect of others and for gaining positions of influence in the community. It, too, however, often changes the actions of the person, not those around the spell-caster.

Odel is good for gaining an inheritance, making a good marriage or other partnership, and for improving family matters and dynastic matters, generally.

How you physically carve, etch, paint, or draw these runes as talismans will depend on your skills as a craftsman or artist. For many people, lack of skills will dictate a small piece of cardboard with coloured texter as a first try. In this case, they need only carry it around in a wallet, pocket, or purse and take it out once in a while to look at it. Much of the effect is autosuggestive sure, but it is none the less effective for that. And it has to be admitted that the tradition that a magician should make all his or her own tools emerged when skills were widespread enough that this was practical advice.

However, there is a technique that you may wish to use that is not very difficult and could provide you with amazingly effective talismans. Start by buying a wood carving set from an art shop or hardware store. You should also get some paints that are permanent and suitable for wood, some small discs of any wood (but a wood sacred to runecraft if you can), some glue, and some metal discs the exact diameter of the wood discs.

Carve your chosen talisman into one of the wooden discs. For example, let's take the case of someone who's not doing well at work. She feels she has been passed over for promotion, and others of less talent have got higher positions. Her immediate objective, then, is to get promoted. This comes under wynn for gaining favour from those higher up, and under isa for gaining promotion itself. Let's say she decides to make a talisman of isa.

She takes one of the discs and, in pencil, outlines isa exactly as she wishes to carve it into the wood, and has taken care to look to the grain of wood. She takes out her straight-edged chisel and a hammer and taps gently until she has made an outline of the rune she wants. She can now add a border to her talisman in the same way. What she does then is take the curved chisel and taps out the shape of the rune taking the stroke in the right direction and reciting her incantation for each tap she makes.

The talisman, by the way, has to be held down with G-clamps or similar device. The details of carving are not important to this work, since they can be picked up from a book or experience.

Once the talisman is carved, it has to be painted. Taking black paint, she would paint the carved rune, again following the instructions given in chapter four. When she has finished this, she would consecrate the talisman, which is discussed in a later chapter, and that would be the end of the matter.

However, she can do more than this. She can improve the value of the talisman without complicating the design of it—which would also complicate the carving job. For example, she could add wynn to gain the support of those higher up. This could be vital to her chances. People are not always promoted because of talent or simple hard work. Sometimes they are compromise candidates. Again, if they are promoted without support from above, they can quickly be bound into no-win situations. This woman will want some allies when she gets up in the world.

She would then take a second disc and carve wynn into it in the same way she carved isa into the other disc. When she has finished she glues the still-unconsecrated discs to the two sides of one of the metal discs, with their runes outermost. What she has then looks something like the diagram shown in figure 7.1.

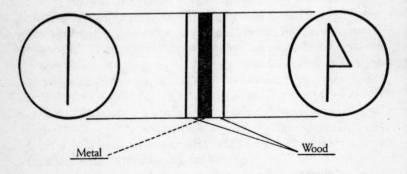

Figure 7.1

This is in fact an orgone energy collector as adapted to talismans. It can work with any sort of symbolism, not simply the runes. For all systems it in fact will pick up some magical energy before it is even consecrated, and will keep its charge longer than a normal talisman.

Moreover, while charged it will draw on the two sorts of energies and reconcile them. A talisman with obverse and reverse dedicated to different events without the layered organic-inorganic material would not do this. So, in this case, the collector will take on the forces of wynn and the forces of isa and combine them to create a promotion which is considered proper and gains the support of superiors in the company.

The same technique can be used in a wide variety of ways. For example, combining the runes os and nyd we can aid successful public speaking, to win debates or convince people to action. If we combine boerc and nyd we can boost the strength of someone critically ill. Again, we can use this technique for quite complicated problems, because the layers do not have to be limited to three.

Indeed, a whole string of runes can be placed on separate discs in a lengthened talisman. Equally, the runes can be placed on the side of a sort of wand with layers of metal and wood, with each layer of wood containing a rune. This 'wand', though, would have a very specific purpose and would not be useful for general ritual work.

For example, we can combine tyr (to gain will) ken (to find the knowledge), ehwis (with aid), wynn (from those in power), and manu (to gain knowledge of ourselves). These can be combined as a talismanic device, as shown in figure 7.2.

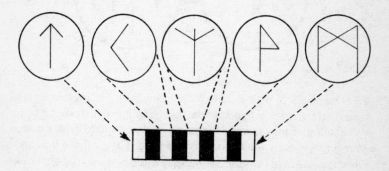

Figure 7.2

Or as a wand, as shown in figure 7.3.

Figure 7.3

When problems become quite entangled, and we need a large number of runes to cover all aspects of it, there are a couple of alternatives open to us. We can refine the problem, of course, but this does not always mean a reduction in the number of runes we need. We can use extended orgone collectors or complicate the symbols used on the talisman faces, themselves. This complication, though, has the advantage that it does not preclude any use of orgone collectors in the talismans.

For example, the runes used in the above example could be combined to form the talisman shown below in figure 7.4.

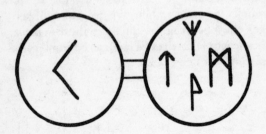

Figure 7.4

Just as talismans of mainstream Western magic can combine text and symbol, so the magical figures of the gods mentioned in the last chapter can be included in talismans. For example, if we wanted to go through adversity, we might dedicate a talisman to Thor, whose prodigial stubbornness could be quite handy. In this talisman we might not only use the runes but Thor's hammer symbol.

Since the circle is a universal symbol of talismanic shape, we could use that for the shape of our talisman. On one side we would have the image of the hammer and an appropriate inscription around the edges, and on the other side the name 'Thor' in runes with an appropriate inscription around the edge of that side. The inscriptions we will use are, 'I am strong in adversity, I triumph' on the obverse and 'Thy hammer mjollnir defends me' on the reverse. It isn't necessary that we put these inscriptions in an ancient Germanic tongue like Gothic, so the resulting talisman we have is shown in figure 7.5

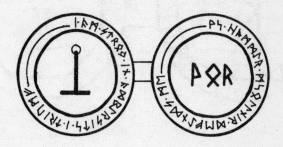

Figure 7.5

A wide variety of talismans can be made using only this basic formula, and in figure 7.6 we have some examples using common topics for talismans. These designs aren't the only ones possible, and the reader should use his or her own imagination. You should note, however, that each talisman may be dedicated to any one of a number of deities, since their functions overlapped. Do not, however, attempt to combine the influences of two different gods on the same talisman by way of combining different symbols. Pick only one deity, but choose it carefully.

In choosing a deity for a talisman, you should always examine from what angle the deity gained a particular attribute. In figure 7.6, above, there is a talisman to inspire poetry, dedicated to Odin. We could have just as easily done one dedicated to Balder. Odin is a god of the dead, and the dead were thought to know things the living did not.

Health

Inspiring Poetry (Odin)

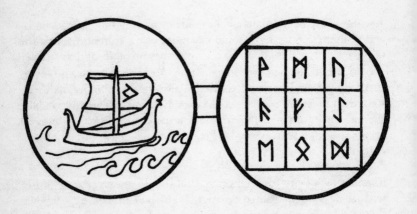

Figure 7.6

Obtaining Justice

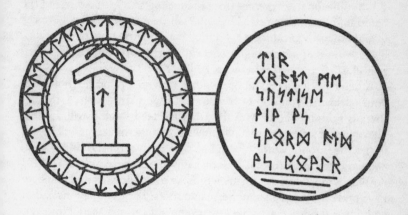

Prosperity

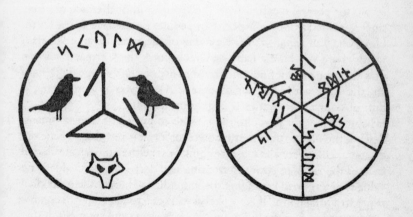

The myth in which Odin gave men that inspiration was where he stole mead made from dead man's blood. Balder is a god of the morning sky, and his poetry emerges from the feeling of a spring day and the entertainments of a court. Thus, the talisman under Odin's auspices would normally produce a brooding, dark poetry. One dedicated to Balder would produce a light, cheerful, perhaps transcendant poetry that glorifies the natural aspects of life.

When devising a maxim or invocation to go around the border of your talismans, you do not have to use a Germanic tongue, though there is nothing wrong with this, transliterated English will do fine. I have seen it suggested that, when writing something that will be put in the runes, only words of Anglo-Saxon derivation should be used, and words adapted from Greek or Latin should be avoided. There is nothing wrong with this, many words we use which have a Latin base have perfect equivalents in Germanic roots. For example, instead of equinox and solstice, we might use evennight and sunstead. However, this is not a vital part of talismanic design. Indeed, what do you do with a word like power—is it from the Anglo-Norman *poer*, or the Latin *posse*? And if it is Anglo-Norman, is that okay? The centrality of linguistic magic for communication with the group soul of the race has long since vanished from the majority of peoples on the face of the Earth. However, you can always use a name of the rune for an equivalent word where you have a Latin or Greek word, the Germanic version of which you cannot find. Otherwise, a use of a fairly large dictionary and thesaurus with etymological notes can keep you on a proper track. But, of course, the matter is largely up to you.

More important, I would think, is the colouring of your talismans. Beyond the use of runes in their own colour, it is possible to generate a general colour for the talisman. Simply take the numerical value of each of the runes in your inscriptions, and derive a single value. The value is determined by adding the individual values of the individual runes to a total figure. If (as is likely) you get a total greater than nine, you have to add up the individual digits to get a single number. If that total is greater than nine, repeat the process until you have a one-digit answer. Take an example:

ᛁ ᚠᚨᚾᛏ ᛊᚲᛁ ᛚᛚ ᛁᛏ ᛗᛃᛊ ᛏᚱ ᚺᛄᛊ

I want skill in mytrade
3+ 8+4+2+1+ 8+6+3+5+5+ 3+2+ 4+4+ 1+5+4+8+5+ = 81
8+1 = 9

Once you have the basic number, you will know what colour the
background of the talisman is. Where, as above, the number is nine,
the background will be grey. Where it is any other number, you have
to decide which aettir the talisman belongs to. The concerns of the
aettirs were given in the chapter on divination, but for convenience
they are:

Freyja's aettir—love, life, and happiness.
Heimdall's aettir—acheivement, money, power, victory, and success.
Tiwaz's aettir—justice, spiritual achievement, and understanding.

Find the rune corresponding to the number of the talisman in the
appropriate aettir, and the colour of that rune will be the colour of
the background of the talisman. For example, a talisman for happiness
with a value of four would be purple because the fourth rune in Freyja's
aettir is os, which is purple.

Both sides of the talisman have the same background colour, and
all runes of maxims are used in determining the background. Any runes
which serve as symbols, however, are excluded from this process. When
you have the background colour, all the symbols and runes are coloured
the complimentary colour. Since works on colour symbolism abound,
we won't go into the matter here. Below is a list of complimentary
colours.

Black is compliment to white
Red is compliment to green
Orange is compliment to blue
Yellow is compliment to purple

The exception is when the background is grey. Then each rune is
painted in its natural colour, and the symbols of the deity are painted

the colour of the rune with which that deity is associated.

There is yet another form of talisman design to which the runes are ideally suited, and that is the monogram. In recent decades there has been a revival of this form of magic with Austin Osman Spare's 'alphabet of desire'. However, though Spare is often credited with designing the system, it was in common use in Europe and the Byzantine Empire both for mundane and, less certainly, magical purposes.

A monogram is made by combining various runes into a pleasing, single form. The runes may be chosen for their esoteric meanings or their use in particular words (such as of an incantation). Since runes are angular it is often very easy to slot one into the shape of another. For example, suppose we want a rune to protect our property—property as odel and protection from tyr. The monogram we design might look as follows in figure 7.7.

Figure 7.7

Alternatively, we could use runes odel and eolh, in which case we might get the monograms of figure 7.8.

Figure 7.8

Monograms can be much more complicated than this, of course. Moreover, the position of a rune in a monogram has no necessary connection with its chronological order in a word, spell or magical formula. Indeed, you can form a monogram from a single rune. In figure 7.9 we have eolh as meaning 'protection to all four quarters'.

Figure 7.9

Take a more complicated example: the individual (manu) witnessing the sun (sighel) rising over the waters (lagu) and banishing (eolh) the dark and cold (hoel). Figure 7.10.

Figure 7.10

The numerical value of a monogram is derived in exactly the same way as mentioned above. The whole monogram is then coloured in that colour or, if you're using something other than a white sheet of paper, you can colour the background of the talisman the numerical colour and the monogram itself in the complimentary colour. If the value is nine and the background grey, the rune itself is achromatic. It will be white on a dark grey background and black on a light grey background.

The exception mentioned above is when a monogram is derived from the runes of a maxim. Since repeated runes are excised, only the value of the runes actually used are taken. Take the maxim, 'I want skill in my trade'. When we use it for a monogram rather than put it on the edge of a talisman, we knock out duplicate letters. What we have left is IWANTSKLMYRDE, and it is the numerical value of this you use when deciding how to colour your monogram.

With a bit of practice it is possible to produce quite beautiful and effective magical monograms. In addition to the points outlined above, there are a couple things to mention which can be used to enhance your design of monograms. For one, it is possible to help organize your runes with a lozenge or a cross, indeed, you can even use a symbol like Thor's hammer or Odin's valknut. Both the cross and the lozenges are used in figure 7.11. The lozenge is the diamond shape in the middle, this is what Charlemagne himself drew, the rest having to be drawn by a scribe. Charlemagne was completely illiterate.

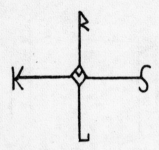

Figure 7.11

For magical purposes it is often useful to have a monogram based on your own (magical) name. This monogram can be used when opening or closing your temple, and can be put at the door as a guard. The power doesn't last long, though, and must be regularly renewed.

Let's take an example of a monogram organized this way. The easiest method, of course, is to take a cross and put the various runes you need on the four ends. To return to an earlier example, suppose we want our property protected, and wish to use odel, tyr, and eolh. We might get one of the examples shown in figure 7.12.

These sorts of device are essential when working with large numbers of runes. Again, let's turn back to an earlier example like 'I want skill in my trade'. In this we will use eight spokes to separate out the

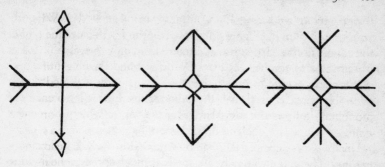

Figure 7.12

thirteen runes we are using. What we get is the monogram shown in figure 7.13. Note that runes don't have to face a particular direction in relation to the spokes or the direction of the sheet of paper you're using.

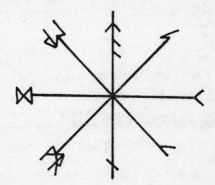

Figure 7.13

We should also note that the same number of runes do not have to be placed on each stem or arm of a cross, though careful consideration should be given to which runes goes where. In the monogram in figure 7.13 for example, doerg and ken, being powerful runes for good, are by themselves on the horizontal stems of the monogram to emphasize their power in the monogram. Combining manu and rad on the south-west stem, I then put sighel on its own on the north-east stem. Thus the connections with death are countered and only the valuable forces of rad remain, emphasis is placed on travel and learning.

It is also possible to emphasize any one rune by making it larger or visibly more central than the other runes. In this latter case the monogram follows the same laws as mandalas, in which the central point or image is a declaration of becoming.

Finally, we can create a talisman by writing down whole incantations in runes. These, quite literally, are 'spells' as much as they are talismans, and the runes are ideally suited to this purpose. Indeed, it parallels the tradition that the Christian Lord's Prayer is effective magical protection when written down and carried on the person. Again, the runic colour schemes can be used when writing these spells. Since the process should be quite obvious, one example will serve to illustrate.

> *By the power of Freyer,*
> *sworn on the silver ring,*
> *I call on the Vanir*
> *to grant unto me*
> *peace and fullness and wealth*
> *that I may give to my family.*

In runes this is as follows.

Figure 7.14

The numerical value of this incantation is 446, which reduces to a value of five. Since the purpose of this incantation, given in the last line, is happiness, it belongs to Freyja's aettir and is coloured black. Thus, the background will be black and the runes white. Once made it can be carried around with you and work that way, or it can be stored in a special place.

Lastly, a couple of notes about transliteration from the Roman alphabet into the Germanic futhark. First, never forget that the voiceless 'th' and 'ng' have individual runes, so do not make 'th' into tyr-hoel but thorn. Second, 'c's should be phonetically converted into 's' (sighel) or 'k' (ken). Third, since there is no 'v' in the futhark, use 'b' (boerc).

You may also wish to simplify the spelling of your incantations and maxims when contructing your talismans. There is nothing wrong with this if it suits your purposes. However, you must take care to spell given names, like mjollnir, properly. If you do simplify the spelling, be aware it is the runes carved that gather the forces, and the resulting difference in numerical value-colour will have some affect on your spell.

Consecration

When your talisman is constructed, it will have to be ritually consecrated. The effectiveness of this consecration will depend on your training and power more than the complexity of the rite. However, to begin, you should have a place set aside for the consecration. This does not have to be a separate temple, though it is best to have one if you can. But a corner of a room, chosen intuitively, will usually do fine.

Place the talisman to be consecrated on a table or other raised surface. It should be possible to walk entirely around the talisman without bending over or ducking your head. A chair should be placed a little distance from the talisman, so you can face it while sitting down. The chair should conform to the same standards given in the last chapter for a chair for your godform exercises.

When you're sitting comfortably in your chair, begin your rhythmic breathing and close your eyes. Imagine you are standing on a structure that can cross worlds. It is woven of a substance that you have never seen before, but which most closely resembles (though it is not) metal.

Flames leap up along the sides of the structure, and the flames are red and gold and blue. This, you quickly see, is a natural effect of the structure itself, and the structure is not being consumed. The structure itself also reflects these colours of the flames. You are, of course, standing on bifrost, the rainbow bridge which serves as one of the paths between the realms of gods and men. Over your head are the stars, and millions of miles below you are the Earth and Luna. And though you are in space, you are breathing your rhythmic breath without trouble.

Continue walking along the bifrost away from Earth. Drink in the sights of this thing, a wonder of its own. Feel the flame giving to you its own energy. It burns away that which is impure and strengthens that which is good. And the further away you get from the Earth, the better, the stronger, the more purified you feel.

There will come a point at which you must stay. You cannot walk further, not through exhaustion, but through some impalpable barrier. When you reach this point, do not struggle to go further, but recite the following.

> *Of fate and power I now speak,*
> *to the Norns I now entreat*
> *to cause the gods to grant that*
> *I shall be pure to my task.*
> *Urd, Verthandi, and Skuld,*
> *I call yea upon the names of*
> *the Vanir, the Aesir, and the light elves.*
> *Grant me the use of this power,*
> *to consecrate the talisman to my purpose.*
> *I seek that it* [state purpose of talisman]
> *so that I may* [state desired result]
> *under the auspices of* [state god of talisman or 'thyselves']
> *and to this end I offer* [state offering].

The offering may simply be part of getting what you want. For example, to get wealth you may offer the work you will do to gain that money. Alternatively, you can make a specific donation such as an offering of a specific sum to charity (and no deducting it from your tax form), a specific task completed, or a specific devotional act to the gods—building a temple or certain rites of worship.

When you have recited the above, open your eyes and stand up. Walk over to the talisman and walk once clockwise around it. At all times, point at the talisman with your right hand. You should, during this, feel a tingling in your fingers and your palm, this is good, and indicates some magical power is flowing.

When you've completed one circuit, inscribe in the air over the talisman the symbol of the god or goddess you have chosen to consecrate the talisman to. For example, the hammer of Thor or the ship of Freyer. When inscribing this, imagine a line of white light being inscribed into the air by the tip of your finger. When you've finished you should ideally see the whole image quite clearly.

If you are consecrating the talisman to the Norns, you should inscribe a circle the plane of which is parallel to the ground, and from the edge of that circle a line straight down but not reaching to the talisman itself. This represents the Well of Urd, where the gods gathered each day to make their judgements of men.

When you have consecrated the power into the talisman this way, you should recite the following dedication.

> *By the life and the powers*
> *I do dedicate this talisman to my purposes.*
> *By the gods of the Aesir and the Vanir*
> *I do charge thee, in order that thou shalt*
> [state purpose of talisman].
> *So said, so be it.*

Please note that 'thee' and 'thou' are not affectations. The word 'you' is too ambiguous for magic, since it is not clear whether a single or multiple party is being addressed. Please also make certain you visualize what you want the talisman to do for you while you state its purpose.

When this is done, go back to the chair and sit down. Close your eyes and return to the bifrost and walk back towards the Earth. When you get to the point where you first entered the bifrost, transfer your consciousness to the physical plane. Coincide with this world with an act of will. When you open your eyes, recite the following.

To the gods and the powers
hail and farewell,
for you have given me
this consecrated talisman
and for that I thank you.

Take the talisman and put it in a small sack of cloth. The cloth should, if possible, be the colour of the background of the talisman. Otherwise, white, black, or blue are best. The best cloths are linen, wool, or cotton. Don't use a synthetic. When the talisman is away, put it far away from the table. Then walk around the table anticlockwise with one hand pointing to the table. Imagine the image you inscribed in the air rising up, through the ceiling, along the path of bifrost, and returning to the gods.

Only then can you cease your rhythmic breath.

Those familiar with ritual magic can, of course, modify this ritual to suit their particular needs. It is, however, quite suitable for the purpose of consecrating talismans. However, there is much more to ritual magic than this, and it is to ritual magic that we turn next.

CHAPTER EIGHT

Ritual Magic

If you are going to practise runic magic seriously, you will have to master more than the symbols, themselves. Above all else, you will have to master yourself and, through that, master a knowledge of the laws of the universe. Each school of magic has a slightly different interpretation of these laws, but these differences are in emphasis rather than the main thrust of the laws. Before describing the techniques, then, we should begin with some suitable exercises and a quick look at some aspects of those laws.

Exercises

Visualization
This faculty is a key to much runic magic. Without it the other skills in magic can come very much to nought. You will have to be able to visualize the various runes, monograms, god symbols, and godforms to perfection. In some cases you will have to be able to visualize the image until it is indistinguishable from something hanging in space in front of you or is actually tattooed on your skin. Only then will the full power of the runes be available to you.

For this exercise you'll need a blank space to practise on. This can be a blank space of a wall (preferably but not essentially white) or a piece of cardboard from an artist's supply shop. A heavy white board, again, is preferable. There should be no patterning on it as there is on some types of railroad board or thin paper like onion skin. When you've got the appropriate board, tape or bluetack it to a wall. Don't use staples, drawing pins, or nails; this ruins the symmetry of the space you'll be using and you'll find your attention drawn to the little pegs.

Your workspace should be at eye level when you stand, so that when you face it, you will look straight into its centre. Many suggest that you put it at eye level when sitting, however, I have found it best to be a bit uncomfortable doing this exercise. If you start your practice under ideal conditions, you'll find yourself unable to practise in less than ideal conditions when practical work has to be done. This limits your magic.

Stand about a metre to a metre-and-a-half from the space you've set for yourself. Relax a bit and begin to trace a shape on your space with your mind's eye. To begin with, you can use your fingers and hands to help you.

Raise your arm out and extend one finger. Slowly inscribe a regular, simple geometric shape into the air—like a triangle. As your finger moves, imagine a trail of light following it and remaining in the air as your finger moves. When it has traced the whole triangle, take your hand away so that there is no light-trail behind it. A triangle should not be hanging in space somewhere between you, your workspace, and infinity.

Whatever you do, don't take your eyes away from the triangle. Simply bring your hand up and retrace the thing backwards. This time, the trail of light should disappear as you press your finger across it. Make certain that you erase the whole of the triangle, even if you couldn't see it at all as you traced it.

This is a point to remember; you will always have to erase the images you trace. At this stage in training, you should not leave magical energy 'unattended' or it will disperse. And if you look away for whatever reason and the image isn't there when you look back, specifically erase the image where you last saw it. Then purify the area where you work. A purification rite is given later in the chapter.

When you've worked with one shape and become proficient at it, change to another shape. If you've used a triangle, switch to a circle, a square, a rectangle, and so on. Just keep it to simple, two-dimensional figures. No dodecahedrons, tetrahedrons or strange squiggles.

Continue the exercise daily. If possible, carry it out at the same time each day. Keep developing the force until it is as concrete for you as something that hangs in front of you physically. For example, you should notice if your finger does not trace a straight line or if the angles of a square are uneven or if the circle is oblong. Work hard at correcting these faults until both your visualization and artwork are mastered.

At this point you will begin tracing shapes in your mind only, if you haven't already begun to do so. Create a point of light which you can control just as precisely and carefully as you control your finger. This sounds little different, but in fact it is infinitely harder. You will need to get it to draw shapes with the precision and clarity you had with your finger. What you will find, though, is that the point of light will have a habit of skipping around the place. When you try to draw a triangle down and to the right, it will suddenly make a loop up and to the left.

If the point does go on like this and draws an extra loop or even a shape totally unlike the one you intended, always erase what is really in front of you, not what you intended. If you find it particularly difficult to erase, use a finger again, but don't get dependent on this.

Some people have trouble making the light go away. If you have that problem, take a nap. That never fails.

Through all this, remember not to try too hard. The jumping point of light can often (but not always) mean you're too tense and are trying too hard. If you feel a tenseness around the eyes, the back of the head, or the shoulders, you will be best served if you consciously relax your muscles and then go on with your exercises. You'll be surprised how much easier control is after that. However, jumping light can also mean simple lack of control and you'll have to practise—for that problem there's no other cure.

When you've gone through these stages of the exercise, start tracing a shape and turning your attention elsewhere for short periods. To start with, just look away quickly and then look back again. The image should be right where you left it. If it isn't concentrate and it should return. If it doesn't, erase where it should be and purify the area.

As the practice continues, you'll dismiss the image further and further from your conscious mind. You'll have to walk out of the room, come back, and then see it. Over time this will give you great control over what you're doing magically. It will result in greater control over yourself, and this will in fact manifest itself in your daily life.

When you get this far, you should extend your control further. Shift the images in space, summon them, dismiss them, and control them in size without having to use your hands, you can then go on to visualizing runes. This, by itself, is a form of rune magic and can be quite useful.

To start, just create the image of the rune as you have other shapes. When you can do that, inscribe the runes in the air using the formulas given in chapter four. In doing that you will be summoning the power of the rune, itself. That is, by using the designated order and direction of strokes and making the correct recitations you will have raised that rune's power.

The power is still undirected, of course. You can then direct it by an affirmation of intent. For example, to complete a painting under inspiration, you could create an ethereal talisman of os. When the rune is completed, point your hand towards it and recite your talismanic affirmation, e.g. 'I will have the magic to finish this canvas with the skill and beauty of a master'.

The ethereal talisman would then remain where it is (in the studio where you're painting, preferably) until the day's work has been finished. The rune would then be erased per normal procedure, but with a farewell of benefice so the energies summoned were returned to their normal sphere of existence.

To make this sort of magic most effective you will have to complete the other exercises. However, at this stage in your development you should have enough power to make it advisable to limit yourself to positive runes like ken and manu and avoid runes like poerdh and thorn. Once you've got this far with visualization you should go on to training your magical memory.

Memory

For this exercise you will need an object that is small and patterned in some way. A Rubik's Cube is ideal for this. You will also need a chair next to a table and a counter next to the table. You can use other objects, but the requisites are that you be able to sit at one surface and that the other surface be higher than the one at which you will sit. You should be able to put the object on the highest surface without bending at the waist.

Start by sitting down with the cube and memorizing it. Examine the different ways the colours relate to one another. In this it is best that the puzzle of the cube be solved (however one does that) and each side is of one colour. This way you can examine which colour is on the opposite side of white, what's opposed to blue, green, yellow, etc. Check if any of the tags are off kilter. Go over each detail of the cube in your mind, fixing it in your memory.

When you've done this, put the cube on the counter and close your eyes. Visualize the cube there on the counter. Move around it in your mind's eye to see every side of it. Make the image in your mind correspond to the real thing on the counter. Check your memory against the reality by opening your eyes every once in a while. If you notice any defect in your visualization, correct it and close your eyes again.

As time goes on you should need to look at the cube itself less and less. If you practise daily you should soon be able to put the cube on the counter and conjure it up in every detail without error no matter how you've positioned it. It will take a long time for this degree of skill, though, and there will be days when you find it harder to visualize than others—a sort of waxing and waning—this isn't backsliding, it's normal.

From the very first time you undertake this exercise, you have to go from this first step to the next. Having memorized the cube as best you can, carefully and consciously pick up the cube from the counter, put it on the table, and sit in the chair. Then close your eyes and imagine the cube again. Now remember every aspect of putting the cube from the counter to table *backwards*.

Remember how your muscles moved, remember what you saw as you watched the cube moving. However, in this phase, it isn't detail that's of prime importance, it's chronology. Start from when you closed your eyes and move back from sitting down to putting the cube on the table and so on. When you've done that, reverse it and remember everything forwards again. Keep putting as much detail as you can in this. Remember not only sights, but sounds and feelings, internal thoughts and all. Get down to details like remembering the feel of the breeze of moving on the hairs on the backs of your hands. Feel the cube in your hands. Everything.

Run this imagining backwards and forwards a few times. Get the feel of the images. Make them seem real, as if they were happening to you again and again. When you've finished this, go on to the next step of the exercise. Again, do this from the very first time you try the exercise.

Summon the cube again, only this time as if it existed all by itself. When you've done that, begin manipulating the cube. Turn it over, make it grow, make it shrink. If you can, look at it from two different directions at once. This last one is difficult and not everyone can do it, but it is highly valuable to those who can.

In this phase, if you can't remember some aspect of what the cube looks like, don't open your eyes. You can go back to it another time. When you've finished manipulating the cube, dismiss the image and open your eyes.

This exercise should be practised until all its phases are under control. It can take a long time to finish a whole session, so never start when you are tired, distressed, angry, or depressed. If you start to feel tired in the middle of the exercise, persevere, you'll soon get a second wind. If your thoughts stray uncontrollably, however, end the exercise immediately.

When doing this exercise, you will work with one main object. However, it's a good idea to change the object you work with every once in a while. If you normally use the Rubik's Cube, you may wish to change to a child's block for a few sessions. Other good objects are a mechanical pencil, a paperback book, a letter opener, and so on. You should also change the counter and table where you normally practise, and where you place the object. Put it in the middle of the counter or table, then the edge, then closer to one side than the other. These sorts of changes ensure that what you are reacting to is what is in front of you and not what your memory has dragged up from previous days. Once you have this exercise under control, it will be time to strengthen your magical will.

Will

Magical will is more than the ability to resist sweets or other temptations. Nor is it self-immolation from uncontrolled asceticism. Magical will is a function of concentration, a control of the self in which a single thought or image is able to transform the transtemporal self. When using the runes in magic, their forces must spread throughout you until all the minor pockets of energy in you converge upon the single element of change. To do this, each of those pockets, like your central core, must be in reach of your will.

To develop this takes many people a lifetime, if not several lifetimes. But the elementary exercises are quite easy to do. Start by taking a small piece of cardboard and cutting it into a regular shape such as you used when visualizing shapes. The cardboard can be almost any colour apart from grey, white, or one of the pastels. Make sure it's vibrant; arterial red, emerald green, and so on.

When you've got the shape, paste it onto a larger piece of white cardboard so the shape is in the centre of the board. The size of this is up to you, but the whole can be the size of a regular playing card without much trouble. The reason you paste one piece of cardboard on another is simply that this is the easiest way to avoid brushstrokes, which can be distracting. However, if you're skilled with an airbrush, by all means go ahead and use it.

When you have your board ready, put it a comfortable distance from you, so you can take in the whole of the shape without shifting your eyes at all. To check this is so, look at the centre of the shape and see if the whole of the shape is in focus—don't budge even one tiny muscle when doing this. If the whole image isn't as clear as a bell, take it a bit further back. Note that it doesn't matter if you're standing or sitting for this exercise, it is only the view of the card that is vital.

When you're ready, simply concentrate on the card. Think of the shape and nothing else. This means not shifting your eyes to anything else, though they can shift over the image itself. It means no verbal thoughts in your head, no voices of what you have to pick up from the shops or what somebody said yesterday or what happened twenty years ago. You must flood your entire being with nothing but the image; that shape in that colour at that time.

When you first start you will no doubt immediately feel something in the back of you resisting. This is often a sign of tense muscles. The normal reaction is to counter this resistance with overpowering force. Since the power of the resistance is fed by your own efforts, this is self-defeating. Simply consciously relax your muscles. The object of this exercise is to get the powers flowing through you, not to bash things.

You may also quickly find that every time you start the exercise you get the urge to scratch, twitch, and wriggle. These feelings you do have to resist. Keep still during the whole exercise.

To aid this, set up a rhythmic breath if you feel you need to. Though it is a temporary distraction, it soon gets put out of mind and then you can get on with your exercise, free of the problems of distractions.

If you continue this exercise every day you will soon find moments when your only thought is that image in front of you. These moments will not be long, but once you achieve it you can go on to the next stage of training the magical will.

For this phase, you'll do best if you get comfortable. Sit down or lie down, remove all restrictive clothing, put a light blanket over you if it's a bit chilly. Take a deep breath and close your eyes and set up your rhythmic breath. When you've done this, begin.

Imagine a seed under ground. Pick a seed you know and are familiar with, like an acorn or a maple. When you have the image fixed firmly in your mind, begin to imagine the whole life cycle of that plant. See the first root spread underground, watch as the stem is pushing up to the surface, through the grass and into the sunlight. See the first leaf emerge. Watch the tree grow, put forth leaves, go through winters and summers, rain and drought. Watch it grow old and die.

During the whole of this exercise, let no other kind of thought enter into your mind. You can let an internal voice explain the action, if you like. If you've learned a bit of botany, you can examine the tree in microscopic detail, watching as the water enters the root hair, flows up by capillary action, is subjected to photosynthesis, and so on. You can examine the birds and insects that live on the tree. And so on. So long as the thoughts relate to that basic theme of the tree, they are okay.

Over time, you should be able to reduce the number of thoughts that run through your mind to only a few. With that, you must begin narrowing the central theme down to the tree itself. Reduce the number of seasons and stages you put the tree through. When you've mastered this, you can go on to the next phase.

For this phase, you will need an alarm and a string of beads. From now on, when doing this exercise, if you have a break in your train of thoughts, move along the string by one bead. When the alarm goes, you can then keep score of how many breaks you've had in your exercise. Start with a period of five minutes, and then work through ten and up to fifteen. When you can go five minutes without one bead passing under your fingers, and can go fifteen without more than four passing your fingers, you'll be ready to go on to magical trance. There is, however, a further stage not essential to mastering the runes.

You can go on to stare at one shape for fifteen minutes, with the object of being able to have absolutely no stray thoughts during that period. For this, start with five minutes, again, and go forward a few minutes at a time as you get better. Though not essential, it can be a most advantageous degree of skill to have.

Trance

Trance has attracted a good deal of nonsense, much of it showing the repressed fears or hopes of the writers involved. But if we look at our lack of knowledge of trance states closely, we are best served if we only state: A trance is a state of consciousness which can be induced which is neither normal consciousness nor dreaming, and is separate from trauma, dysfunction, or unconsciousness. It has many known variants typified by intensification of one or more known aspects of ordinary consciousness. These include suggestibility, concentration, dissociation from the physical body, perception, and conjunction of conscious and non-conscious aspects of the psyche.

And that, by and large, is about all our scientific knowledge of trance states. Since science has not yet distilled 'conscious' into a physical correlate, this should not surprise us. But occultists have always accepted what scientists cannot admit—not everything has a physical explanation. Since the existence of consciousness has always been accepted by occultists, they have never had any qualms about putting trance states to use. In this sense the technology of trance use of the shamans would match anything known by today's scientists.

For this work we'll concentrate on a single, simple method of self-hypnosis. It was chosen for its simplicity, ease of use, and safety.

When starting out with this exercise, you will have to get comfortable. However, as practice progresses, try to be able to put yourself into a trance state when under more and more difficult conditions. Your aim should be to be able to put yourself into a trance and to be able to control that trance at any time and in any place.

Once you are comfortable, all you will have to do is tell yourself you are going into a trance. You will then count from ten to zero while reinforcing the message that you will enter into a trance. This simple process works for a great many people simply because non-ordinary states of consciousness are not as far away from our day-to-day existence as we might like to think. A script for entering a trance can be as follows.

I am now going to put myself in a trance. It will be an easy thing to do. I will be perfectly safe while in my trance and will be able to end my trance any time I wish. I only have to count from ten to zero, and when I reach zero I will be in my trance.

Ten. . .nine. . .eight. . .I am now moving from the normal state of consciousness. Seven. . .six. . .five. . .I am now entering my trance state. Four. . .three. . .two . . .I am in my trance, I am feeling the nature of my consciousness change. One . . .I am in my trance, and the state is getting stronger. Zero. . .I am in my trance state now.

If you wish, you can add a physical signal to this, to show that you really are entering a light trance. For example, you can make your arm rise, apparently of its own accord. It will, of course, be your muscles doing the work, but the signal is none the less potent for that. Simply add to the script the appropriate references to the signal. For example, as below.

I am now going to put myself into a trance. It will be an easy thing to do. I will be perfectly safe in my trance and will be able to end my trance any time I wish. As I enter this trance, my [right or left] arm will rise into the air by itself. I will now count from ten to zero, and when I reach zero, I shall be in my trance and my arm will have raised itself over my head.

Ten. . .nine. . .eight. . .I am now moving from my normal state of consciousness. My arm already feels lighter, lighter, lighter. The weight is just disappearing from it. Seven. . .six. . .five. . .I am now entering my trance state. My arm is rising from [my leg/the armrest/etc.]. Four. . .three. . .two. . .I am in my trance, I am feeling the nature of my consciousness change. My arm feels light, as if it were made of helium-filled ballons. My arm is rising, rising, rising. It is already moving over my head. One. . .I am in my trance, and the state is getting stronger. My arm is now floating over my head it is so light. Zero. . .I am in my trance state now, and my arm returns to its place as my trance settles in.

If your arm doesn't rise on the first try, and even if you fail to enter a verifiable trance right away, do not be discouraged. Much success may be foiled simply by inhibitions about trances which many people have. Gentle persuasion in the form of practice does much more than trying to break down doors by insistence. If you try the exercise daily and vary it a bit to keep it fresh, you will eventually succeed. In fact, over time you will need less and less of a lead up to the trance. It will be possible to enter your trance with no more than, 'I will now enter my trance, I am now entering my trance, I have now entered my trance.'

From the very first, whether you feel you have entered a trance state or not, you will have to end that trance. This is one of the universals of the occult—what you invoke, you dismiss. Only the end effect of a spell or trance is allowed to continue when your work is finished. In this case, you simply end the trance much as you entered it. A script might go much like this.

I have now completed my work. I am now going to leave my trance and return to daily consciousness. I shall be happy, healthy, shall meet the nicest people, and enjoy all forms of success. I will now count from zero to ten, and when I reach ten I will be in normal, daily consciousness. Zero. . .one. . .two. . .I am now moving from my trance state of consciousness. Three. . .four. . .five. . .I am now entering normal consciousness. Six. . .seven. . .eight. . .I am in normal consciousness, the trance state has slipped away. Nine. . .I am now in normal consciousness, and am ready to complete all that I need or want to do. Ten. . .I am fully ready, the trance is gone completely, I am in healthy, normal, daily consciousness.

The repetitions of health, success, and 'normal' consciousness are not indications that the trance is not any of those things. Indeed, the script for entering the trance could also include these references. However, trance provides access to and requires energy from the non-conscious elements of the psyche. When these commands are provided at the termination of the trance, it gives the psyche a new impetus to improvement and helps keep a 'head of steam' in the non-conscious aspects of the self. We all need goals for health and happiness, the close of each trance should reinforce this for us.

When you have mastered all these exercises, you will be ready to begin practical work in magic. But to do this work properly, you will have to understand some of the laws of magic.

The Laws of Magic

I've described how Germanic myths seem to have an underlying structure from Indo-Iranian myth, and that what has been handed down to us is a degenerate form of the myths the Germanic pagans actually believed in. These suggestions are not unique to this work, though no occultist has sought to combine these factors to a restoration of the original aspects of the myth. Moreover, it is from this understanding that we can know the laws of runic magic, and without it, any but the most minor magics will fail to be used to best effect. For those who wish to delve deeply into this subject, I offer a few words and the suggestion to read the various myths from an esoteric point of view.

In Germanic paganism, as in Mithrasism and Zoroastrianism, there are two separate and dichotomous forces in the universe. In Zoroastrianism these forces are good and evil. In Mithrasism and paganism, the differences are less sharp. For example, the gods and giants had different origins in the void. They were separate powers entirely, and never had need to merge, though they eventually did so by marriage and other interactions.

As in Zoroastrianism there are many levels to the pagan reality, and the world we know is one place among many. Energies, forces, deities, and heroes could pass from one sphere to another, changing the nature of the whole to a greater or lesser extent. To the Zoroastrian, the birth of Zoroaster himself is one such infusion, and shall give rise to three later infusions of similar divine beings each of whom is descended from Zoroaster himself. Mithras' own killing of the bull was a similar infusion for Mithrasians. In Germanic mythology, the death of Balder was such an infusion, not into our world, but the realm of the dead. One who was at the highest came to the lowest. Heimdall's creation of human society was another such infusion. In all three religions the practice of magic or religion is a similar such case.

For the pagans as the Zoroastrians and Mithrasists, balance is an important aspect of these infusions. In runic lore this is expressed in the affirmation, 'a gift demands a gift'. We ran into it during the discussion on divination, and should now examine another aspect of it.

When you undertake magic you call on certain energies. To balance those energies you will have to return undifferentiated energies to the same forces you draw from. In other words, there are two sorts of spells—the ones that build up energy and the ones that use it to obtain certain effects. Too many of the latter and not enough of the former lead to a breaking up of the links to the higher powers. Thus, if you have any major works of magic in store, you will have to build up energy.

This same rule of ecology has another effect. Just as in your divination, you will have to have the whole of the picture in your mind when you undertake magic. You will have to know where you are drawing your energy from and whence to return it when you are through. Essentially, these forces come from the gods of Asgard and Vanaheim. Sometimes you will have to take them from those who are not quite gods, such as the Norns. In these cases you must return the energy in full to the correct deity as described in chapter six, the godforms.

This is not a hard thing to do, and I've spent this long on it in order to emphasize it. Far too many works on magic provide one side of the matter and not the other. Both must be understood if runic magic is to be successful.

There are other, practical laws of magic that must be obeyed. These are quite simple to keep in mind and need not cause undue problems.

To begin, isolate where you are working. All forms of magic isolate the place of working in different ways. Western magic draws a circle, Egyptian magic uses talismans on the magician, and Germanic paganism had its sacred site. In this case, we will use an identifiable place of work (set the limits carefully in your mind) and use protective runes in the four cardinal directions to protect it. We look at this a bit later.

When working, always have an identifiable beginning and end. Conclude your work, dismiss the powers. Return the energies that have not been used to their proper realm with thanks. But have a distinctive completion to the work.

When you are deciding on a magical intent, understand the whole of the matter. If you want to use magic to, say, become a writer, you'd better have a pretty good idea what type of writer you want to be; journalist, columnist, freelancer, etc. Be certain what sort of material you want to write, what hours you will work, and so on. Unlike other forms of magic, which create a 'next step' result, the runes need a more complete pattern to work from. They need to know where the final balance will turn up. This means that when your magic is successful, you will have to use another rite to close down the operation. The runes won't do this by themselves, they will continue to work for you and create a sort of overload—too high, too hard, too fast.

However, this same sort of detail of blueprint makes it unlikely the runes will achieve what you want in a form of which you had no inkling and no desire. It also means you can apply the runes to more short-term effects than other sorts of magic. The need to balance led Dion Fortune to write that general success is acceptable as a magic goal, it is white, but a specific success makes the spell black magic. In the runes, that accounting has been done for you.

Indeed, you may realize during a rite what it is you will have to provide to achieve what you want. You will then be able to back out of things before the bill is presented, as it were. This advantage is not provided by all types of magic.

These are the basic laws you must always keep in mind, and they are not arduous. It does mean you will have to consider what you are doing, but in all forms of magic premeditation is essential to performing any spell. We will now go on to some practical methods of rune magic, starting with skrying.

Skrying

Skrying is more than a method of divination, it is a means of contacting the higher forces from which you will gain your powers. It is a neutral case, supplying almost exactly as much energy as it draws, so that the balance is maintained. It is thus an excellent start to any practise of magic.

To perform the rite, you'll need a bowl or goblet, a table, a chair, and either some water or some wine. Water is acceptable if you are using an opaque vessel, but if it is of clear glass you'll have to use wine, and red wine at that.

Put the bowl and wine on the table, and then project a protective rune to each of the four quarters. Several runes would be suitable, but ken is a good choice. Since it represents a torch and initiation, it is good for protecting a place where illumination is sought.

To the Germanic pagans, the four quarters are where Odin and his two brothers put dwarfs who held up the skull which was the night sky. We can thus incorporate them into the rite. Begin by inscribing ken to the north. They should be done as described in chapter four. When ken has been set, intone the following.

Nordi of the north,
see thee the light of the torch,
Accept its flame,
and let none pass you by,
lest it scorch them to death.

Then turn to the east and perform the same charge for Austri, then to the south and charge Sudri, and to the west to charge Vestri. You begin in the north because this is the direction of holiness for the Germanic pagans. Their second most holy direction was the east, where the sun rose. When this is done, your next step will be to purify the wine and bowl. For this you will have to use the runes wynn and doerg.

Stand by the table where you've put the bottle and the bowl. Over the bowl etch the rune wynn and recite the following.

> *By the wynn,*
> *I purify you.*

You can, of course, substitute a word like 'glory' for the name of the rune, but this makes little difference to the spell.

When you've purified the bowl, pour the *unpurified* wine into the bowl. This will be purified with doerg. Etch this rune over the bowl so that it is facing the surface of the wine. You should now have over the bowl the monogram in figure 8.1.

Figure 8.1

When you've done this, recite the following.

> *By the power of day,*
> *and of the wynn,*
> *I purify all that lies this way.*

Next, you will have to employ a new technique. You'll have to call down a power not of the runes, and project it through an established runic force. To do this, choose a particular godform (in this case, we'll use Freyja) and project the power through an ethereal talisman.

Simply assume the godform of the deity in question and put your hands towards the etheric talisman. Let the energy run out your fingertips, pass through the talisman, and enter the object you've directed it to, now carrying the desire you entered into the talisman. The only thing that should be in your conscious mind is that talisman. It must engulf you.

If you do not feel confident at using a particular godform, a specially-designed prayer or invocation will do the same. The formula for these prayers is easy to understand. Simply be certain to call upon the deity to smile on your project from their great realm. Then the major attributes of the deity are mentioned, and how the deity is related to the function of skrying. For example, if you were calling upon Odin, you might mention Valaskjal, his seat of all-seeingness. When calling upon Freyja, you would mention specifically that she is a seeress. For example:

> *Freyja, mighty seer of the Vanir,*
> *bestow favour upon my spell,*
> *Like a cat sees in the dark,*
> *thou peerest through veils of life and death.*
> *Bestow favour upon my spell,*
> *grant me thy knowledge,*
> *grant me thy power,*
> *bring thy power to bear,*
> *upon this vision.*

Then allow the power to flow through your fingertips as has been described above.

When this has been done, sit down and look into the bowl of wine. Perform something like your exercise of will, but fill your mind with nothing but the surface of the wine. After a short period you will find the wine beginning to black over, becoming less of a surface and more of a doorway. When the whole of the surface has thus changed, an image or images will seem to emerge. Initially, particularly if you haven't mastered your exercises, the images will mean nothing, or at best very little. They're a sort of 'junk' that has to be cleared before you can skry effectively. However, with practice, these images cease and others take their place. Not everyone gets all the same types or in the same order, but roughly the images start with junk, then to symbolic images that can only be recognized when the event in question is passed, then symbolic images that can be understood, then concrete images, and then, sometimes, deep images that go beyond simple skrying itself. But no matter what level, all skryers get a day when nothing seems to make sense.

To ensure accuracy of prediction, always keep a record of what images you saw and what predictions you made from them. You would be surprised how many people, when faced with a situation, will make two very different predictions and only remember the successful one.

When you have received all your images, you will have to close your rite. Since we've used the godform of Freyja—which, by the way, is not limited to females—it is to her realms you return the energy. If you have used the godform, drop that and recite the following. If you have prayed, simply recite the following.

From Freyja I was given the power,
to Freyja I now return it.
Hail and farewell to thee,
Goddess and seeress.

Next, erase the runes you etched over the bowl. Since doerg was raised second, this is the first to be erased. Then erase wynn. With each, return the energy to its origin, with thanks. Then take down the wards you set. In each case, erase the rune ken and recite the following to the appropriate dwarf.

Nordi of the north,
I take back the light of the torch,
and give it to where it belongs.
You let none pass you by
and for that I thank you.

Then return the energy of ken to its original source. This is done by the same recitation as has been mentioned. Repeat the closing formulas for east, south, and west, in that order.

With that the only thing left do so is dispose of the wine. The best way is to pour it onto soil as a libation to the earth, or into a river or creek as a libation to the sea. If you need to pour it down a sink, though, this is less of a disaster than some would suggest. Simply regard it as spreading holiness to the lowest of levels.

Skrying is a good practice, since it helps your skills in projection. When you've mastered that skill you can begin to practise the skill of etheric talismans.

Etheric Talismans

There's one thing to remember about etheric talismans; they are very energy-consuming. Their over-use will quickly diminish your powers. They can exhaust you not only magically, but physically, leaving you fatigued, listless, and drained. However, used properly they are an ideal method of magic in some situations. They have a great deal of power and can be used quickly. They are flexible yet specific, and as long as you recharge your sources, they are highly useful.

The basic method is to etch the rune into the space of your will and then empower that rune to a particular effect. For example, suppose you wish to protect yourself from something, and choose the rune eolh to do this. Simply imagine a bluish-white light in front of you (and you can use your finger if you have to) which traces a vertical line straight up, while it does this you recite, 'By my sword'. Then the bluish-white light should trace the left diagonal up and to the left while you recite, 'and my magic'. Then the right diagonal up and to the right while you recite, 'I am defended'. This will give you the rune eolh in bluish-white in front of you, so that it can now be retraced in purple.

Trace the vertical line from bottom to top, so that the purple light totally replaces the former bluish-white light. Again, you can use your finger for tracing. While you trace, you should recite, 'By my sword'. Then the right diagonal is traced down and to the left while you recite, 'and my magic'. Then the left diagonal is traced down and to the right while you recite, 'I am defended'. The rune will now be etched and should rest before you. It should have the full power you are capable of endowing it with.

You should now enter your trance state and, if possible, take on the appropriate godform. When that is done, you then charge the rune with its duties. For example:

Eolh, thy power is great,
Give me the use of that strength,
Defend me against mine enemies,
Both seen and unseen,
Both open and hidden.

During this time you should have in mind the specific thing or person the rune should protect you from. When it has done its work, return it to you and erase it, sending the forces back to where they have come from. You should add thanks to this, for example:

Oh, eolh, you have aided me.
I am free of danger now.
I return you to [the Aesir, Vanir, etc.]
With thanks and farewell.

If you are far from where you etched the rune, imagine yourself being where you summoned that rune. Visualize the background in all possible detail, and erase the rune as if you were standing there. This will erase the original rune.

This sort of etheric talisman is quite a useful tool, but it can also be extended by the use of monograms. Indeed, you can use the cross and the lozenge to separate the runes and make the runes easier to visualize. However, remember that the more complex the design the harder it will be to visualize the whole strongly and accurately. It is best to practise with single runes and perfect them before moving on to monograms.

There are two methods of building monograms. You can etch the whole monogram in its appropriate colour or build the individual runes and shift them in your mind until they link up into a single monogram which then has to be re-etched in its own colour. With a great deal of practice, you can just visualize the whole monogram at once, but this takes great expertise and is not recommended.

Design the monogram in the way described in the chapter on talismans. Suppose, for example, we want to use the simple monogram designed to protect property. You'll remember it was made of the runes tyr and odel, and is shown in figure 8.2.

Figure 8.2

It's number is eight and we'll assign it to Tiwaz's aettir, so the colour of the monogram is yellow. However, the original runes are red and brown. If we want to etch the individual runes, we would do this as follows.

There's no single 'right' order in which to etch the runes. We can go from the most important to the least important, we can use alphabetical order, or simply move along the monogram taking each rune in turn. I prefer to have a narrative device in my order, so we will start with odel and move to tyr.

We etch odel in the normal way with the methods given in chapter four. Trace the rune in bluish-white and then in brown. When that's done, tyr is etched, again, in the normal way, in the space occupied by odel. Tyr is etched in exactly the way the monogram requires. Again, we trace the rune in bluish-white and then in red. That done, the whole of the monogram is etched again in yellow. This yellow trace will totally replace the red and brown colours of the original runes.

When tracing a monogram there is no specific order in which the strokes should be retraced. The monogram is not simply the combination of two runes, since their interaction creates a new aspect to the monogram. However, you may wish to start with common areas first and then go on to other strokes. In the above monogram this would mean colouring the central vertical first and then the various diagonal strokes. However, this is a matter where your own intuition will have to guide you.

When colouring the monogram yellow you may recite the original lines for etching the individual runes, or can use the strokes as the basis of a recitation that will charge the monogram with its purpose. This will save you from reciting a charge after the monogram is complete. I would point out, though, that during the whole of this etching you should have in mind as much of the task you have for the rune as you can. Only thoughts relating to that should be allowed in your mind.

Suppose you specifically wish to prevent your house from being broken into. You might recite the following as you colour your monogram yellow.

| *Justice and power*
↑ *I need you*
↑ *To defend what is mine,*
↟ *My home and my goods*
↟ *Will be defended*
↟ *From all forms*
↟ *Of attack.*

When the monogram has completed its work, it will have to be erased just as are individual runes. To do this you must strip back the colour of the monogram, erasing it stroke by stroke. This may be done in reverse order in which the strokes were done, but though this is helpful it isn't essential. When the monogram is stripped back to the original colours of the runes they are erased in the normal way. If you only etched the monogram in bluish-white light, this is erased stroke by stroke. Again, if you are far away from the monogram when it's time to erase it, visualize the place where you created it and then erase it. You will also have to give the remaining energies back to where they came from, and give thanks when you do.

If you are using a cross or lozenge in your monogram, this, too, is etched and erased. The first etching colour is always bluish-white, and it is always erased directly, there is no 'natural' colour for it to revert to.

When you've gained skill in etheric talismans, you will be ready to go on to the use of ritual implements.

Ritual Implements

From a variety of sources, we can build a fairly comprehensive picture of the ceremonial life of the Germanic pagans, particularly the Norse but extending back to the late Bronze Age. Carvings on caves, when correlated with myths, folk beliefs, and archaeology give a picture of an unbroken tradition that lasted until recent times and perhaps still continues, today. Specific aspects of this ceremonial life, however, still have to be filled in. For example, we know very little of the ritual worship of the twin gods (the Aclis). But even with these gaps, we still know enough about Germanic pagan ritual to know its basic magical structures and to put those structures into use today.

The Wand
Like many cultures, the tribes made use of the magic wand, and had a good number of names for it. In size the wand could be anything from a walking staff to a small piece of wood the length from the heel of the magician's palm to the end of their middle finger. It might be straight or forked.

To construct a wand yourself, you will need a rod of hazel or ash. If these are unavailable, you will need a fairly sturdy wood; a wooden arrowshaft is often a good subtitute. The length of the wand should be in proportion to your own body; from fingertip to the heel of the palm, from fingertip to the end of the elbow, or the height of you plus the width of four fingers at the third joint.

When you have your wand cut, take a sharp knife (such as from the kit you bought to make your talismans) and scrape a small flat side to the wand. Into this you should etch and colour your runes in the same way you would for a talisman. Which runes you choose are up to you, and they can be chosen for symbolic purposes, according to a magic formula, or as an incantation. I would, however, recommend you put your own name into the runes, whether it be your given name or a magical name chosen for runic work. You may also wish to dedicate the wand to the power of a particular god. For example, you may wish to dedicate the wand to Thor. The formula would then be bound on either side by the sign of the hammer of Thor or a swastika, and you might wish to use the formula, 'In the name of Thor'. In this case, we'd have something like figure 8.3.

Figure 8.3

When you've carved the wand, it will have to be consecrated.

To do this, start by clearing an area as you did for skrying. When your wards are set up, project the runes of Freyja's aettir, one by one, into the wand. As you project each rune, recite as follows.

Feoh—I have come bearing gifts
Ur—and shall face the dangers
Thorn—of my enemies.
Os—But by inspiration
Rad—I undertake the journey
Ken—into the cave of shamans/shamankas
Gyfu—to receive the gift of this wand
Wynn—and return with the magic it holds.

When you've recited this, wrap the wand in cloth, preferably white linen. If linen is unavailable, try cotton. Just never use synthetic cloth of any sort. When the wand is put away, go back and close the ritual as you did to close skrying.

This same consecration ritual can be done for all other implements.

Drinking horn or cauldron

Skrying can be done with almost any bowl or cup, but it is useful to have a special vessel for both this and sacred drinks. The cauldron and the drinking horn both relate to a ritual of drinking, which was important to the pagan tribes as to all cultures of this world, including our own. Indeed, one myth shows the Vanir and Aesir brewing ale as part of a sacred oath, and in the *Lokasenna*, Loki taunts Odin by saying he, Odin, had once vowed never to take a drink unless it was with Loki. The drinking horn and the cauldron are powerful tools, but they aren't synonymous. The horn is the brotherhood, the cauldron is the generative powers of woman. Your own gender, however, does not determine which tool you will find most effective, and it is best if you can use both.

In either case the vessel will be made of metal or glass, though the latter is harder to cut. Around the rim of the vessel must be the appropriate runes. Again, the message is up to you. It is suggested that part of the invocation be a bar to poison which, although hardly likely to be necessary, has a force of tradition behind it.

The cauldron will have to have an identifiable neck on which the runes can be placed, and should have three small legs rather like a Celtic cromlech. The body of the cauldron should be as round as possible.

The drinking horn should fit comfortably in one hand and should contain rather more than you can drain in a single draught and never less than about two cups of liquid. It should have a stand in which it rests or two small legs on one side so that, with the tail, it can be left filled but unattended. It must come down to a point and must not have a base like a cup or tumbler.

Since the shamans were travellers they carried little that was not light and physically practical. However, as time went on and Germanic society became more settled other ritual implements were used to denote the various gods and to adorn their temples. The primary interpretation of the wand, cauldron and horn are father, mother, and child, but there are a number of other devices you may wish to use.

Thong

Whether made of rope or leather a thong represents the binding force of a god. Both Odin and Tiwaz (significantly) employed these among their followers. It can be a simple length of leather or rope with a knot at one end to prevent it escaping the loop at the other. In this way the thong will always be a loop, representing not only binding force, but eternity. You can also wear the loop around your waist when performing runic magic in order to symbolize your devotion to a particular god or eternity itself.

Necklace

A string of beads can be useful, as in the case of the magical exercise of will. It also counts the number of times you do a prayer to ensure you do that prayer a prescribed and magically significant number of times. To be fully in the pagan tradition, it should be amber beads strung together. Since this could be expensive, a set of wooden beads may suffice.

A Ring

Best made of silver, this would be an arm-ring on which runes of a binding oath would be etched but not coloured. This would be worn on the arm during a rite or laid upon the altar when an oath is being made. If silver is the problem, a suitable base alloy can be substituted. There are a number of jewellers throughout the world who'd be able to fashion and etch the ring. One suggested runic inscription would be, 'By Freyer, Thor, and Njord I am bound by my oath.' In runes

ᛍ·ᛒᚼ·ᚠᚱᛗᚼᛗᚱ·ᚦᛟᚱ·ᚨᛁᛞ·ᛏᚿᛟᚱᛞ·ᛁ·ᚨᛗ·ᛒᛟᚿᛞ·ᛍ

Figure 8.4

this is shown in figure 8.4. The opening and closing symbols might be Thor's hammer, Freyer's boat or a wave of Njord.

Altar

The altar has less importance among the Germanic pagans as it has in the Middle East, where the Semetic religions developed. However, an altar is still a valuable item in a place of magical work. If possible it should be placed upon the ground, not a concrete floor. In a small grove or under a thatched roof would be ideal but these are hard to come by.

The essentials of the altar are that a pillar be placed on either side of it. These must be made of wood and should be somewhat thicker than a hand can normally surround with thumb touching middle finger. These pillars should be placed on either side of and behind the altar.

The altar itself should be about the height of your belt buckle or just a bit higher. It, too, should be made of wood and the longer side should face you as you approach it.

There should be a place on your altar for a holy flame, and this can be a candle or an altar brazier. Other than that the tools will vary from time to time, and depending on the rite you are doing or the god you are working with.

Though the altar itself should be plain the pillars behind it can be carved and painted as ornately and intricately as you can manage. You can also drive iron nails into it as this, with some flint and tinder, can be used to start fires. There is a myth in which Thor has a piece of whetstone lodged in his head and the myth seems to have reflected a ritual purpose, probably initiation.

Where possible, if you are working with a particular deity, their symbol or image should be on the altar. For Thor have a hammer (not a claw hammer but a throwing weapon). For Frigg have a goblet. And so on.

When you have all these you will have the tools needed for ritual magic. Remember before I said rune magic is ecological. To draw down the power, power must be entered into the egregore. This sort of ritual magic will ensure you do not drain those forces. In addition, it can actually boost the effectiveness of your magic. Skrying at an alter has an advantage to skrying at a card table, and there is more to it than simple atmosphere.

For example, an etheric talisman etched over an altar will have the energies of that place reinforcing its attempts to complete its charge. The place of the altar becomes a charge of residual energy. This being the case it becomes useful to have a simple rite, devotion, or energy storage, as you prefer.

Devotion

Stand in front of the altar with all items ranged upon it. At the very least there should be your wand, your binding thong, and your drinking horn or cauldron or, preferably, both. If the cauldron is too heavy it can be left on the floor. You should be wearing your arm-ring on your left arm.

Approach the altar, as you stand before it should be facing north. Stand with your feet together and raise your arms in salutation. Your palms should be facing the altar with your fingers together, your elbow slightly flexed. Your whole body should be relaxed but alert. Recite the following.

> *Gods of the Aesir,*
> *Gods of the Vanir,*
> *Warriors against strife,*
> *Hallowers of the daylight.*
> *Grant me that I follow the right way,*
> *And accept what the Norns*
> *Have meeted out to me.*

Take your wand and point it to the north. Inscribe your protective rune into the air and then go on to complete the setting of wards for the other cardinal directions. Your wand will eventually become a reserve of power in its own right for this rite.

Next, place the wand on the altar and with the runes doerg and wynn purify the drink in your horn or cauldron. Light the candle or brazier with the words:

Wise Mimir, I need your aid
to light my way with your wisdom

Enter into your trance state. If you are devoting yourself to a particular god in this rite, place their symbol to the four quarters. For example, in a rite of Thor, do the hammer to the four quarters. For Odin, use the valknut. For Freyja use the sign of the boar, and so on.

At this stage, if you have any prayers to address to the deity, do them now. When they are done, put your hands to the north with the palms out and press undifferentiated energy in that direction. If there are no prayers, do this after setting the symbol of the god to the four quarters.

Next, perform the sign of the god or, if you prefer, the hammer, over the cauldron or horn. Despite the fact the hammer is attributed to Thor, it can be used as a neutral blessing since all the deities depended on Thor's hammer in the myths and all have a hallowing function such as Thor derived from his hammer. Now drink from the horn—wine or ale will do. If you are using a cauldron, naturally use a ladle which is draped across the lip. If you have a congregation of any sort, this is the time they are addressed or any activity regarding them is completed.

When the rite is finished, begin closing the rite by smothering the candle or brazier while reciting the following.

I thank thee, Mimir,
for the aid thou hast given me.

Erase the runes to the four quarters and thank the dwarfs who have guarded you. Do not erase the signs of the deity. Then turn to the north and say:

By this magic
I have made
Midgard and all the realms
Safe and free.
I have stored the magic
That I may call upon another time.

You can then store away your various magical implements. By performing this devotion once a week you should be certain of having the power you need for whatever runes you wish to call on. Moreover, it provides the basis for further magical work, for example the magical incantations which are used as talismans can be used as affirmations at this altar.

Incantations

Above all else the runes are associated with written magic. Once you've begun using your altar you can make use of this aspect of the runes without difficulty. Simply compose a magical invocation that achieves your intention (just as you did with a talisman) and recite it in a magical rite. For example, suppose you want to become wealthy in this financial year. The same rules apply to a magical intent as apply to forming a divinatory question—we would then narrow the intent to gaining £125,000 in the next twelve months which will be achieved by business and commerce. In this we include starting and developing a business, stocks and bonds, and so on.

With the intent clear, we choose an appropriate god to whom the spell is addressed—in this case the candidates are Odin, Thor, Freyer, and Njord. Of these, Odin is most concerned with inherited wealth, Thor is a protector of trade and commerce, Freyer is concerned with wealth through plenty, and Njord is a god of commerce. Of these, Thor and Njord seem the most likely, and since we've dealt with Thor, we will invoke Njord for this charm. The invocation might go as follows.

Njord of the seas,
Defender of commerce and cargoes.
Give me the magic and the power
By which I might become wealthy.
In the next twelve months,
I wish to have £125,000
By trade and cargo.

The runes don't have a real number system of their own, not one that can handle numbers of the hundreds of thousands. We can use words or Arabic numbers, although numbers adds a discordant note, so if we transliterate this charm, we'll use words. If you use the numeric value of the runes, you have to add the value of the runes together, and there are a lot of 8's in 125,000. When the charm is transliterated and the colour discovered, we're ready for our ritual.

Light the candle or brazier on the altar and set your wards to each of the four cardinal directions. Then towards the ceiling and below you use the symbol of the god Njord. This is either a boat or an arch, and is used in exactly the same way Thor's hammer is used. For this, see figure 8.5.

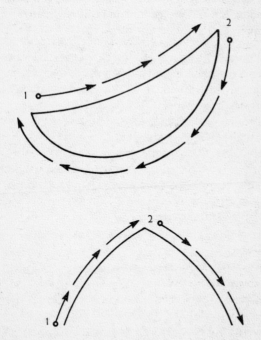

Figure 8.5

Now stand at the altar facing north and recite your charm. With each rune of a word, visualize that rune forming and see it retreating to higher realms. There is no need to use the strokes, simply visualize the whole of the rune in the complimentary colour of the background of the charm.

When you have completed the charm, thank the deity for his generosity and close the ritual as normal.

This charm, like the other rituals, can be extended through various methods. However you should now have the skill to understand how this is done and to have a general feel for runic magic. Indeed, if you have completed all the exercises and know all the runes thoroughly, you should be able to practise this sort of magic quite successfully. The only other significant aspect of magic which you have to learn about by reading is astral projection, and this is what we explore in the next chapter.

CHAPTER NINE

Astral Projection

Traces of the practice of astral projection are rare in Germanic mythology, though it is well known as an occult technique of shamans throughout the world. But, though a well-kept secret among certain initiates for centuries, the traces still remain in the mythology. For example, both Freyja and Frigga were said to have 'feather' or 'hawk' forms, and the use of these forms is very similar to what we would call astral projection. That Loki 'borrows' the forms is not a bar to this, oft times when one person cannot project, magical aid from another will boost their abilities so that they can project.

Nevertheless the runes, like the *I Ching* and the Tarot, make excellent doorways and a study of their use in this way can be valuable when using them in general magic.

For those who have not practised astral projection or are new to the occult, a few words of explanation. The modern methods of practice can be laid at the door of S.L. MacGregor-Mathers, who helped found the Hermetic Order of the Golden Dawn last century. Before his time people had found that by skrying in a crystal ball, they felt as if they had been sucked through it and would then experience something that can best be compared to a wakeful dream.

That is they would imagine themselves to be experiencing events in realms that did not exist on Earth. The scenery was often (but not always) fantastic, and the beings met in these places were often fabulous and included monsters, demons, and angels. The people seeing all this were quite aware of the nature of the vision—i.e. it was a hallucination, not a delusion, in terms of psychology and philosophy. That is, they understood they were sitting in a chair while another part of them was undergoing these circumstances, but the experiences weren't weakened for that. Moreover, unlike a dream, these people weren't passive in this state. The lack of free will that characterizes all but a few dreams was never in evidence in these visions. Not only that, the vision could be terminated at will.

That so many people started experiencing the same phenomena, often spontaneously and without prior knowledge of other people's experiences' created a sensation among spiritualist circles. (And provides some evidence for the concept of planetary initiation.) But the method provided serious drawbacks, particularly that it was impossible to control to what realm the individual went. This meant it was impossible to consistently explore certain areas of the astral world. Moreover, it led to people meeting entities whose nature they did not know and whose benevolence or at least neutrality was open to doubt.

MacGregor-Mathers solved these problems by the technique of astral doorways. The basic technique is to take a symbol and stare at it until it seems to flash. Then close your eyes and see if the symbol remains, though in a complimentary colour. By an act of will, revert it to its correct colour and imagine it being painted on a door or embroidered in a curtain. Imagine yourself going through that door or curtain. You will then find yourself in the astral plane. More, what you experience will have a real and verifiable relationship to the symbol you passed through.

In other words, take a symbol and fill your self with it as per your exercise of magical will. Then follow through with the skills you gained in your exercise of magical memory. The full technique for the runes is as follows.

Technique of Projection

First you have to get comfortable, whether in a chair such as you use for godforms or lying down in a bed. Usually sitting is preferable to lying down, since it's easy to fall asleep in the latter position. When you've made your choice, set your wards around the area and then get comfortable. It is best if you loosen any tight clothing like belts, collars, shoes, etc.

Begin your rhythmic breathing, then go into your trance. When these are established, etch into the space of your will the rune through which you wish to project. When you close your eyes, you should still see the rune.

Now imagine yourself walking the bifrost, the rainbow bridge. The description of this was given in chapter five, but we'll review it here. It is a structure of red, yellow, and blue and is of a material that is not wood, metal, stone or plastic. It is a woven material and the intricate patterning can be seen clearly if you inspect it closely. On the edges of the bridge on either side flames leap up high above you. Above you you can see the stars; they're brighter and more numerous than you have ever seen them before. You are seeing them from space itself and you can see the Earth far below you. The bridge stretches all the way back to the Earth and then forwards further than you can see.

The rune you have chosen should still be in front of you. Follow it as it leads you along the rainbow bridge, taking you further and further from the Earth. Sometimes this can take quite a while, but this need not concern you. While you are in astral form walking does not make you tired, you can follow the rune to its end.

At that end you will see a gate. This gate may seem to be Asgard or a stopping point on the bridge. At this gate you will see the rune inscribed on the door of the gate. With an act of will pass through the gate. When you've passed through you will find yourself in the realm of that rune.

When you want to return from that realm, summon the gateway again and, by passing through the gate, you will again be on the rainbow bridge. You can then return to the physical world.

Always remember to end your trance and erase your wards when you finish.

This is the basic technique, one that can be mastered by almost anyone. It provides a wealth of information about the occult and one's self.

A Sample Projection

What follows is an example of a projection into the rune nyd, performed by myself. It is not the hardest projection I've ever done, in fact things went quite smoothly. This will not always be the case, and that is something you should keep in mind.

I stand on the rainbow bridge and have only a short way to walk before I reach the gateway. This is not at Asgard but a watchtower on the bridge itself. The rune is embossed on the ebony gateway across the bridge. The door opens and I pass through.

I am in a place of very fertile growth. There are fruit and other trees all about me. I think I'm in an orchard until I realize the trees are not set in any pattern. I am simply on the edge of some woods, next to some bushes that grow along the side of a dirt path. In the distance are hills and grass and children playing. Rather than go up to them I turn and walk.

I am dressed as a warrior. There's a sword by my side, a practical tool with a strong blade and a substantial hilt and crossbar. Slightly too large for the blade, perhaps. The scabbard is plain black. I am wearing a metal helmet, from the bit I can see, it's bronze. I am wearing a jerkin and trousers of animal skins and boots which are kept up by thongs of leather. I have a large and heavy cloak of animal skin which is much more worn than the rest of my clothing. Metal rings have been sewn into my jerkin to reinforce it. My scabbard has a heavy belt to it, and the belt is decorated by tooled metal and jewels.

I come upon a young woman of Celtic rather than Germanic derivation, as evidenced by the black hair and blue eyes. She is very beautiful and carries a bowl of fruit and nuts. She's startled by my approach, but when I greet her she returns my greeting and seems considerably eased.

'Who are you?'

'I am a magician'. I use the German *Zauberer* for 'magician', and in fact the whole conversation seems to take place in German, though I've consciously forgotten most of it.

The woman looks at my attire with some suspicion.

'You dress as a warrior.'

I bow slightly and she notices the pommel of my sword. It's a large gem shaped like a diamond but coloured like a ruby. It's begun to glow and, from her expression, this shows I'm something more than a fighter. Perhaps they've had such troubles in this area, lately.

'There is a place nearby where one such as I might have an interest.'

'You mean the house of hell. It is that way.' She points along the way I have been travelling. I thank her and continue on my way.

The walk is long, and during it I keep expecting to be attacked. Surely, there will be something to impede my way? Necessity requires struggle, and struggle requires opponents. Yet here there seems to be nothing and no-one concerned with stopping my achievement, whatever it might be.

With this thought I feel a lightness, and something raises me off the ground. My cloak has become like two great wings and I am carried high into the air.

I watch the landscape below me. It is lush growth, largely wild. The grass is often high and consists mainly of a sort of wild grain. Trees are sparse, as if many years ago there had been a fire through this area— grass always comes back faster than trees.

Around the hills the path continues to wind until I see ahead of me a mountain. This is granite grey and there is little vegetation on it, where the other hills are covered with grass and have softened edges when compared to this outcrop of rock. In the middle of this mountain is what looks like a small hut, but the hut is made of stone and no path leads to or from it. Except for a mountain climber and somebody who flies, there is no way to get to it.

There's a small ledge at the entrance to the hut, and I land on that. As I land I notice two yellow eyes staring out at me from the darkness of the hut itself. There's a dimly heard low growl that makes me realize whatever the thing is, it's large.

I draw my sword.

The pommel glows more and more brightly, and as I step cautiously into the hut, the light is enough to illuminate the small room. I see the eyes belong to some kind of lizard, and then the thing is gone in a second. I stop for a minute, listening and looking hard. Slowly, I step further into the hut.

The symbol of a hut on a mountain is universal. It is a source of wisdom, and astral projection is above all a source of wisdom and knowledge, not an entertainment. I believe that what message this projection has for me will come out of this hut.

The animal suddenly returns and attacks. My hand goes out and catches one claw just before it can rend open my side. Though people are generally immune to horror-show death on the astral plane, the more you open up to it the more vulnerable you are. I should not be in any danger here, but experience has taught me caution. Besides, my hand can almost just reach around the central of its three claws.

It's a clumsy animal, and if I push its claw up high it can't get any other claws or its teeth at me. I'm tempted to stab or hack it with my sword while it's helpless, but for some reason I relent. Using leverage, I manage to manoeuvre it out the doorway through which it barely fits and then over the edge. It falls down the mountain side, rolling here and there and occasionally nearly getting its footing. Though bruised, it's still alive, and though it can climb back it will take some time to do so.

When I turn to the hut again, I see an old man. He wears some kind of woven cloth that looks like burlap or horsehair. His skin is leather and what hair he has left is white, long, and thick.

'What do you seek?'

'I seek necessity and its achievement.'

He seems to know me and the image of the wise old man is certainly one of the universal archetypes catalogued by Jung.

'You have already achieved this'. He points to the sword. 'This is your achievement. Your sword is your oath, and your oath is your necessity. This you have already discovered and I can teach you no more than that'.

He draws the rune nyd on my forehead, and both my physical and astral foreheads begin to tingle. He then asks me what I want to achieve. I tell him my major goal for this year, and he tells me I have all but already achieved it. More, he shows me how it has been and will be done. Taking this lesson, I return through the doorway to the rainbow bridge and from there to the physical plane to erase my wards.

Interpretation

All the foregoing may seem spectacular or simply amusing, as a short morality play or a badly-plotted fantasy, depending on your point of view. But astral projection, like daily life and history, can be interpreted in a mytho-poetic way. In the projection above I sought to discover the core meaning of the rune, only to discover I had it with me. A sword has long been accepted as a symbol of the oath and is so taken in my normal work. And that the wise old man should have taken the oath as the keypoint is in itself significant—as the affirmation of the god whom I follow goes, he 'helps no oath-breakers, liars, or those who shrink from the balance.' He is, by the way, an archer and a swordsman.

Common motifs occur in many projections. A path is one such. The projection achieves its intent best when the person keeps to that path, whether it is a dirt track or the rainbow bridge. There will normally be two guides, a lesser guide (the woman) and a greater guide (the wise old man). The greater guide, who isn't always the vehicle of the central message of the vision, is normally one of the greater or fixed archetypes of magic or Jungian psychology. These can be, for example and to use Jungian terms, the Great Mother in one of her many guises, the Wise Old Man, the Hero, the Divine Child, or Death-Rebirth. In this case it was the Wise Old Man

The Wise Old Man was recognizable not only by his age but by his situation. He had lived as a hermit and was reached after a large lizard, or dragon, had been conquered. Note here that the dragon was in the house of hell. The woman had used the German word, 'holle', which translates as 'hell' but which comes from a word meaning the concealed place or hole. This is exactly what was found.

The dragon (similar to Nidhogg) was my own baser instincts. These were clumsy and the point of the struggle (for me) was not to slay them but to put them aside. What we hate conquers us, and the object is not to slay—and thereby become absorbed by—our lower passions, but to neutralize them. When these passions are no longer a threat but can still be drawn upon, wisdom can come through to the conscious mind.

Once I succeeded in my test—and every projection has a test—the reward is received. That reward is attainment of the vision. In this case the vision was the sound advice of wisdom. In other cases it may be a change in the circumstances in our lives, or some other benefit.

Dangers of Projection

With such value it would seem there must be a cost to projection, some dangers that lurk in all this. According to some writers the dangers are manifold. To others there seem to be no dangers whatsoever, and anyone but anyone can master the technique in a few hours. Neither extreme is the case.

There are costs to astral projection. It takes time to learn and more time to master. The visions you see when you start are often weak or soft and only strengthen after a time. It takes energy and can draw on the magical energies you've stored. And it takes concentration, conscious projection is not to be lightly undertaken.

Moreover, there are some dangers. Some people can become obsessed with the astral plane. They see it as a fantasy realm in which their every wish can come true. They loose sight of the desire for spiritual growth and concentrate on a search for wonders.

And whatever the prevailing view on such things, it is also true that astral projection can bring you face-to-face with your own worst fears. You meet demons, if you want to use that terminology. And the demons aren't funny or unreal; they can do damage. They have real power and you are going to have to overcome them at some point or another in your travels.

But these dangers are minor for most people. Obsession is for the unbalanced. And if there are demons there are guides who seek to bring us to a successful conclusion in our quests. So though we might meet a dragon, we can also meet the Wise Old Man who conquered it long before we even knew it existed.

Astral projection is a technique that will reach its centenary in 1988 or 1989. In that century it has already done much to change the view occultists have of the world. Whether the technique existed in earlier days and Mathers simply released it to the world or whether he truly devised it, that revelation has drastically altered the way we experience the world around us. And as a tool of perception it can be neither ignored nor done without. It is a tool every occultist would do well to know, for the rewards of that knowledge are great.

CHAPTER TEN

Conclusions and Further Considerations

In this book I've tried to give more than a quick picture of the runes, and have tried to provide a context in which the runes operated. I've thus given some attention to the pagan myths and have drawn attention to parallels between this tradition and other traditions. In doing so I've taken a very different course from other works which have concentrated on the runes themselves and have extended interest only as far as Odin or shamanism in general.

I've taken this approach in hopes that a more balanced view of the runes and their magic might prevail. Too often I have found the image of the runes to be of a magical curiosity whose use was eliminated by the Western tradition of magic. This view would ignore the very real and important contributions the runes have to make to occultism.

For example the runes as a divinatory system are better suited to answer some types of questions that the Tarot or *I Ching* answer sketchily. The godforms follow a somewhat different pattern to the Egyptian or Greco-Roman godforms in that the Germanic systems gives the gods a wider scope of concern. There is a wider range of interests filled by each godform, and far from being a 'fuzziness' of overlapping interests, I have found this to be a highly valid way of looking at the forces of the deities. It takes an understanding to know the source of the god's power and how it extends into concerns similar to those of other deities.

For all this we've only scratched the surface of runic lore, and many more things will have to be known to draw the full potential from this form of magic. For example, we would have to know more of the archer and skiing god, Ull. Of the cultic activities of the Germanic pagans.

To discover a preserved pagan temple as we've discovered Mithrea of the Mithrasians. And above all we've got to know the myths as they were understood by the priests when the myths were in their zenith. I have already suggested that we would find the 'doom of the gods' was originally the 'purification of the world'. I would go further and suggest the creation myth, the binding of Fafnir, and ragnarok are, between them, a central mystery play of Germanic paganism. And only when the myths are restored will this come out.

In the meantime the runes have an important role to play in the revival of pagan lore throughout the world. They are a magic that sees the physical world as the result and consequence of spirit, not its antinomy. It is a magical system involved with the things around it. It is part of a tradition that has survived well into our historical period. Indeed, some of the mythic elements of the Germanic pagans seem to have been used in the stories that were compiled and unified into *Le Morte d'Arthur*.

The runes could carry this kind of conviction and can now regain their interest because they represent an understanding of human beings. Its maxims and aphorisms emphasize this again and again. 'A gift demands a gift, better not to pledge than to overpledge, the runes allow a man enough but never too much', 'the path to a friend's house is always straight though he live far away through thick woods'. Simple as they seem, they show a practicality and an individuality that is often lacking in the world we live in. The Germanic pagans understood things we seem to have forgotten. They remembered that no real decision can be made unless it includes a renunciation. They knew that all things remain in balance, and if we expand in one area too fast or too powerfully, other things are lost.

In a world overproud of its technology and its capacity to destroy itself, and the only protestors are those who would consign all we are into being nothing more than the pre-holocaust world, when the number outweighs the man it is assigned to, these sorts of lessons are the very sort we must learn now. That above all makes the runes essential for us today.

Bibliography

I thought of providing an extensive bibliography, but I came to the conclusion a long list would scare away many readers from pursuing the subject further. Those who are determined to read widely on the subject will find extensive bibliographies in *The Norse Myths* and *Gods and Myths of Northern Europe*. In this work I pick the best works in the area mentioned, and can recommend each of them to the reader.

1. General References

Snorri Sturluson; *The Prose Edda*
   A Christian writer of the twelfth century who at least had a sympathy with the pagan deities. Much of our knowledge of the myths comes from this man.

Cornelius Tacitus: *Germania*
   Written in AD 98, this is the longest of contemporary accounts of Germanic society and paganism. Much of the geography and other individual aspects need to be treated with caution.

Saxo Grammaticus; *Gesta Danorum*
   Another significant source of knowledge about the Germanic myths, but this writer was hostile to paganism. It is also a lesser work of literature, and this may have helped push it to obscurity. Is important for an alternative view of Balder as a hero, not a god.

The Elder Edda also called *The Poetic Edda*
   A collection of myths and skaldic poems, highly useful for the kennings or alliterations which abound in Germanic poetry.

Beowulf
   A Saxon poem written with some verve, illuminating the life of the Norse between the sixth and eighth centuries AD.

The above are all available in various translations of even quality. The difference in volumes is normally the notes that accompany the texts and it is up to the reader how they wish to make use of these.

2. Mythology

Auden, W.H. and Paul B. Taylor: *Norse Poems* (The Althlone Press London) 1981
   Draws on a number of sources and has a handy Norse-to-English dictionary.

Branston, Brian: *The Lost Gods of England* (Thames & Hudson, London) 1957
   Good analysis of the Saxon versions of the Germanic gods. Especially interesting is his reconstruction of the role of Tiwaz before the rise of Odin/Wodan/Wotan.

Crossley-Holland; *The Norse Myths* (Penguin, Middlesex, England) 1980
   Narrative retelling of many of the myths in as close to a chronological form as possible. Good bibliography and notes.

Donington, Robert; *Wagner's 'Ring' and its Symbols* (Faber and Faber, London) 1965
   Not directly related to mythology, it does show how Wagner tapped many of the ideas in pagan symbolism.

Ellis-Davidson, H.R.; *Gods and Myths of Northern Europe* (Penguin, Middlesex, England) 1964
   Pagan Scandinavia (Thames & Hudson, London) 1967.
   The first is a standard work on the gods, myths, and cult activities of the Germanic peoples. Good bibliography. Essential.
   The second work concentrates on the Brozen Ages beliefs as exemplified by rock carvings, etc.

Martin, Stanley John; *Ragnarok: An Investigation into the Old Norse Concepts of the Fate of the Gods* (Van Gorcum & Co., Assen, Netherlands) 1972

Though specialized it does help show how the myths we have are not the myths the pagans really believed in.

Ward, Donald; *The Divine Twins: An Indo-European Myth in Germanic Tradition* (University of California Press, Berkely and Los Angeles) 1968

Again, specialized but illuminating of many aspects of Germanic mythology.

3. Zoroastrianism

Boyce, Mary; *Zoroastrians: Their Religious Beliefs and Practices* (Routledge & Kegan Paul, London) 1979

Good introductory work.

Zaehner, R.C.; *The Dawn & Twilight of Zoroastrianism* (Weidenfeld & Nicholson, London) 1961

Again, excellent. Look up his other works on Zoroaster.

4. Mithrasism

NB The study of the god Mitra/Mithra/Mithras is now in upheaval, academically. Particularly the studies of the Western version of the deity. I have therefore chosen a work most suitable to the interests of occultists:

Verna-Seren, M.J.; *Mithras: The Secret God* (Chatto & Windus, London) 1963

Well suited to the interests of occultists, but read widely on the subject if at all.

5. The Runes

Howard, Michael; *The Magic of the Runes: Their Origins and Occult Power* (Samuel Weiser, New York) 1980

The Runes and Other Magical Alphabets (Aquarian Press, Wellingborough, UK) 1978

Two very fine books. The latter shows his research to better effect and is the broader survey. The former is a more practical work of magic.

Koch, Rudolf; *The Book of Signs* (First English Club, London) 1930, reprinted (Dover, New York) undated. Translated by Vyvyan Holland.

Very little relates to the runes, themselves, but the details of monograms and housemarks is useful to the practising occultist.

Thorsson, Eldred; *Futhark: A Handbook of Magic* (Samuel Weiser, York Beach, USA) 1985

Good work from a practitioner of runic magic.

6. Magical Exercises

Bardon, Franz; *Initiation into Hermetics: A Practice to Magic* (Dieter Ruggeberg, Publisher; Wuppertal, West Germany) 1956

A work by an adept.

7. Astral Projection

Brennan, J.H.; *Astral Doorways* (Aquarian Press, Wellingborough, UK) 1971

Beyond a doubt the best work written about projection through symbols.

Denning, Melita and Osborne Philips; *The Llewellyn Practical Guide to Astral Projection* (Llewellyn Publications, St. Paul, USA) 1984

Though more about what I would term etheric projection, the exercises and attitudes of this work are valuable. Denning and Philips have written a number of very good works, some with titles as appalling as this one.

Index

Of related interest . . .

FORTUNE-TELLING BY RUNES

A Guide to Casting and Interpreting the Ancient European Rune Stones

Casting rune stones to shed light on future events is one of the least documented methods of divination and, though runes are wholly European in origin, their use as indicators of fortune is little practised in the West by comparison with such oriental oracles as the *I Ching*.

David and Julia Line set out to redress the balance in this comprehensive, entertaining and practical book, which contains everything you need to know for casting and interpreting individual and group meanings from where the stones fall on a runic chart. Contents include: the history and mythology of the runic alphabet; detailed instructions for preparing and labelling a casting cloth; how to make your own rune stones; casting and reading; in-depth index of nearly 200 individual runic meanings; and sample casts and interpretations.